"*A Course in Miracles* offers me daily inspiration in my life, work, and relationships. In *Holy Shift!*, Robert Holden selects an inspiring mix of aphorisms, meditations, and prayers to help us to live the principles of this great work. Thank you, Robert, for this beautiful gift."

— **Marianne Williamson**, *New York Times* best-selling author of *A Return to Love* and *A Year of Miracles*

"As a faithful student of *A Course in Miracles,* I'm always seeking new ways to experience the text. In Robert Holden's new book, *Holy Shift!,* I've found a wonderful guide. Holden's book is infused with his passion and love for the Course. Each handpicked passage offers readers a simple and powerful framework for experiencing miraculous change. I recommend this book to anyone on a spiritual path."

— **Gabrielle Bernstein**, *New York Times* best-selling author of *May Cause Miracles*

"*Holy Shift!* presents the heart and soul of *A Course in Miracles* in an easy-to-use daybook. Whether you are new to *A Course in Miracles* or a long-term student, *Holy Shift!* is a perfect companion. We recommend that this book sits next to everybody's copy of the Course."

— **Gerald Jampolsky, M.D.,** and **Diane Cirincione, Ph.D.,** authors of *A Mini Course for Life*

"The gift of a lifetime is contained here! The wisdom, poetry, and love imbued in *Holy Shift!* will bless and heal your life. Robert Holden, a true teacher of the path with heart, presents some of the most inspiring passages of *A Course in Miracles* in a clear, touching, and easy-to-receive way. Thank you, Robert, for opening the door to a better life for all of us."

— **Alan Cohen**, author of *A Daily Dose of Sanity*

"*Holy Shift!* is a wonderful compilation of excerpts from the Course that will keep miracle-minded thinking at the front of your awareness. Robert Holden has done a very impressive job of arranging the book in such a way that will encourage more people to practice the essential principles of this spiritual masterpiece. I highly recommend this marvelous book!"

— **Gary Renard**, best-selling author of *The Disappearance of the Universe* trilogy

"I once thought that miracles were reserved for saints and looked something like the stigmata. *Holy Shift!* reminded me that miracles are far more ordinary. A miracle is an inconspicuous moment, an inner triumph, when we choose to release fear, when we forgive, and when we dare to return again to love. My copy of *Holy Shift!* will have love-worn traces of how often I have read it. It's a daily reminder of our most crucial purpose to cultivate our capacity to love."

— **Meggan Watterson**, author of *Reveal*

"Robert Holden has taken the essence and power of *A Course in Miracles* and made it beautifully accessible in *Holy Shift!* This book allows us to practice the core principles of the Course and serves as a great reminder of the power of love in our daily lives."

— **Mike Robbins**, author of *Nothing Changes Until You Do*

"Whether you are new to *A Course in Miracles* or a long-time student, this book will guide you, day by day, to the very essence and heart of the Course. Robert is a wonderful exponent of *ACIM,* and this is his latest valuable contribution."

— **Ian Patrick**, Miracle Network, London

"In *Holy Shift!* Robert has done a fabulous job of skillfully distilling and sharing the heart of *A Course in Miracles* for us in a most beautiful way. Please read, be inspired, and remember who you are and why you are here."

— **Nick Williams**, author of *The Work We Were Born to Do*

"*A Course in Miracles* is a wellspring of Truth that never runs dry. Robert Holden's book, *Holy Shift!,* is a communion of 365 sips from the chalice of this immaculate living well. Welcome to your *Holy Shift!*"

— **Sondra Ray and Markus Ray**, www.liberationbreathing.com

"*Holy Shift!* is a wonderful book. Robert Holden takes what I consider the best spiritual, philosophical, and psychological book in the world and makes it easy and accessible for beginners and veterans alike. I love this man! I love this book!"

— **Chuck Spezzano**, author of *If It Hurts, It Isn't Love*

ALSO BY ROBERT HOLDEN

Books

Authentic Success (formerly titled *Success Intelligence)*
Be Happy
Happiness NOW!
Loveability
Shift Happens!

CDs/DVDs

Be Happy
Coaching Happiness
Follow Your Joy
Happiness NOW!
Loveability
Shift Happens!
Success Intelligence

Flip Calendars

Happiness NOW!
Success NOW!

All of the above are available at your local bookstore,
or may be ordered by visiting:

Hay House USA: www.hayhouse.com®
Hay House Australia: www.hayhouse.com.au
Hay House UK: www.hayhouse.co.uk
Hay House South Africa: www.hayhouse.co.za
Hay House India: www.hayhouse.co.in

HOLY SHIFT!

365 DAILY MEDITATIONS FROM A COURSE IN MIRACLES

EDITED BY
ROBERT HOLDEN, PH.D.

HAY HOUSE, INC.

Carlsbad, California • New York City
London • Sydney • Johannesburg
Vancouver • Hong Kong • New Delhi

Published and distributed in the United States by: Hay House, Inc.: www.hayhouse.com® • *Published and distributed in Australia by:* Hay House Australia Pty. Ltd.: www.hayhouse.com.au • *Published and distributed in the United Kingdom by:* Hay House UK, Ltd.: www .hayhouse.co.uk • *Published and distributed in the Republic of South Africa by:* Hay House SA (Pty), Ltd.: www.hayhouse.co.za • *Distributed in Canada by:* Raincoast Books: www.raincoast.com • *Published in India by:* Hay House Publishers India: www.hayhouse.co.in

Cover design: Michelle Polizzi • Interior design: Riann Bender

A Course in Miracles is published by the Foundation for Inner Peace.

Library of Congress Cataloging-in-Publication Data

Holy shift! : 365 daily meditations from A Course in Miracles / edited by Robert Holden, Ph.D. -- 1st edition.
    pages cm
  ISBN 978-1-4019-4510-7 (hardcover : alk. paper) 1. Course in Miracles. 2. Devotional calendars. I. Holden, Robert, 1965-, editor of compilation.
  BP605.C68H65 2014
  299'.93--dc23

                    2013045638

Tradepaper ISBN: 978-1-4019-4318-3

10 9 8 7 6 5 4 3 2 1
1st edition, April 2014
2nd edition, April 2015

Printed in the United States of America

To Tom Carpenter.
My friend. My mentor. My brother.
Thank you for bringing *A Course in Miracles*
to life for me.

CONTENTS

INTRODUCTION

A Course in Miracles is one of my favorite books. It sits on a bookshelf in my home reserved for spiritual classics like the *Bible*, the *Bhagavad Gita*, the *Dhammapada*, *The Imitation of Christ*, the *Tao Te Ching*, *The Prophet*, the *Masnavi*, and *The Gnostic Gospels*.

I read something from *A Course in Miracles* every day. The Course has been part of my daily spiritual practice for the past 20 years. I take it with me when I travel, on my iPhone and computer. Like all great literature, the more I study it, the better it gets. Whichever page I turn to, the words are always relevant and helpful. I still come across passages that seem brand new, as if they've been downloaded into an edition especially revised for me.

A Course in Miracles is a big book. It's more than 1,200 pages and 500,000 words long, and its size alone is too imposing for many. Also, it's written in old-style Christian English and is full of iambic pentameter, which is the meter that William Shakespeare often used. Each page is infused with a mix of rich prose, spiritual poetry, powerful aphorisms, and beautiful prayers. My hope is that in *Holy Shift!* I give you a taste of this mighty work while still being faithful to its power and grace.

The story of how *A Course in Miracles* was written is a miracle in itself. It involves Helen Schucman and Bill Thetford, both professors of medical psychology at Columbia University's College of Physicians and Surgeons in New York City. Helen described herself as a "psychologist, educator, conservative in theory and atheistic in belief." Bill was the head of her department. They were anything but spiritual, and their relationship was anything but peaceful. One day, Bill declared he was tired and angry about their antagonism and that "there must be another way."

Bill's outburst triggered a chain of events that neither would have predicted. Over the next three months, Helen experienced a series of vivid, highly symbolic dreams. Then, one day, she heard an inner Voice that said, "This is a course in miracles." Helen confided to Bill her most unusual experiences. It made her feel very uncomfortable, but Bill was highly supportive. Over the next seven years, Bill helped Helen to listen to what the Voice had to say. In a short preface to *A Course in Miracles,* Helen says:

> It seemed to be a special assignment I had somehow, somewhere agreed to complete. It represented a truly collaborative venture between Bill and myself, and much of its significance, I am sure, lies in that. I would take down what the Voice "said" and read it to him the next day, and he typed it from my dictation. I expect he had his special assignment too. Without his encouragement and support I would never have been able to fulfill mine. (Preface viii)

Helen Schucman is described as the scribe of *A Course in Miracles.* She did not want her name to appear on the book because the Voice that dictated the words was not her own. So "who" is the Voice? The Voice introduced itself to her as Jesus. Helen struggled with this, but she could not deny the truth and beauty of what she heard. Also, Jesus continually encouraged Helen to see that the purpose of the Course was to direct readers to their own Internal

Teacher—to the Christ in all of us. Helen made sure that at her funeral no mention of the Course was made. She wanted the Course to stand on its own.

What is *A Course in Miracles?* It consists of three books: a 669-page Text, which explains the philosophy of miracles; a 488-page Workbook for Students, which offers 365 daily lessons for living the philosophy; and a 92-page Manual for Teachers, which includes a Clarification of Terms. It also has two supplements: *Psychotherapy* and *The Song of Prayer.* The whole work offers a system of spiritual psychotherapy and an invitation to experience inner peace and freedom.

I began my study of the Course by reading the Text. Initially, I found it difficult to understand. I'd get halfway down a page and be so full of poetry and mind-blowing principles that I could barely stay conscious. I even typed out the Text on my PC in an effort to "get my head around it," so to speak, but that hardly helped. I then switched from the Text to the Manual for Teachers. Here's where I read that, "a universal theology is impossible, but a universal experience is not only possible but necessary." After that, I decided to focus on the daily lessons in the Workbook, and this has been my main focus ever since.

Although the Course is written in Christian language, it is studied by my friends who are Buddhist,

Muslim, Hindu, and Jewish, because it offers a spiritual philosophy that reflects perennial wisdom. I found the Course in an old esoteric bookstore at a mind-body-spirit festival held in Central London. I bought it on a whim because I liked the title and also the idea of miracles. The Course describes a miracle as something you experience when you are willing to shift your perception from a psychology of fear to a psychology of love.

A Course in Miracles encourages you to look at everything afresh. "Instruction in perception is your great need," teaches the Course, in a section of the Text entitled "The Problem and the Answer." The goal of the Course is to help you know yourself. "This is a course on love, because it is about you," it states. It offers a system of mind-training that helps you undo the blocks to love—conditioning, judgment, and fear—so that you can enjoy and participate fully in the miracle of existence.

"There is no conflict that does not entail the single, simple question, 'What am I?'" states the Course. The Course wants you to see that you are more than just a small, separate ego set apart from creation. "You are not an ego," and "you are not a body," says the Course. The body is simply the dress code for the human experience. The *holy shift*, as I call it, is the recognition that you are a spiritual being having a human experience and not a human being who has occasional spiritual experiences. In other words, you don't have a soul; you *are* a soul.

> Holy are you, eternal, free and whole,
> at peace forever in the Heart of God.
>
> —Manual for Teachers. 15. 1:12.

The Course describes the perception of separateness as "a tiny, mad idea" that causes a "great amnesia" that leads you to live "a little life beset with fear." Albert Einstein described separation as "an optical delusion." The Course says, "In you there is no separation." The goal of studying the Text and practicing the lessons in the Workbook is to make an "exchange of separation for salvation." This exchange is described as an *inner shift*.

The Course is a love letter written from your soul to your ego. In this love letter you are asked to let go of your separate self-image, made of pain and fear, in order to experience your wholeness again. Your self-image is full of unworthiness because it is not worthy of you. "You who are beloved of God are wholly blessed," says the Course. You are created whole, there is nothing missing in you, and any unworthiness stems from conditioning and a mistaken identity.

In a section in the Text called "Seek Not Outside Yourself," the Course encourages you to stop searching for the happiness, peace, and love you long for. It's because we believe that happiness is outside of us that we've made the world into a giant shopping mall. It's because we believe that peace is outside that wars are fought every day on this planet. It's because we are looking for love, instead of being the loving presence we truly are, that we live in a world where love is so hard to find.

"There is no world! This is the central thought the course attempts to teach." That's quite a statement. What does it mean? "Your concept of the world depends upon this concept of the self," explains the Course. How you see yourself is how you see the world. For example, if you perceive yourself as separate, then everything you want (like happiness, peace, and love) is also perceived as separate from you. You experience life as "a tiny you and an enormous world." However, when you remember your wholeness, your oneness with everything, the world withholds nothing from you.

"There is no sin," says the Course. Now this really is a holy shift! *A Course in Miracles* states that nothing you do can ruin or alter your holy innocence. No matter how lost you are in the "detour into fear" and no matter how many wounds you experience in your "personal repertory of horrors," your holy innocence remains intact, waiting to be witnessed again. The Course says, "Its central theme is always, 'God's Son is guiltless, and in his innocence is his salvation.'"

"There is no need to suffer," says the Course. Here is another holy shift in perception. The Course invites you to consider the possibility that because God is unconditional love, God does not punish you, cause you pain, or make you suffer (even for a good cause). "And so your innocence has not been lost. You need no healing to be healed," says the Course. Any pain you experience is the pain of the ego and not of your soul. Therefore, all pain is a form of mistaken identity, a call for love, and a prompt to remember who you really are.

How do we experience a holy shift? How do we undo the illusion of separation? How do we experience a Self without guilt? How do we create a world with no war? The ego is a "poor choice as a teacher," the Course says, because it never sees the big picture. "Resign now as your own teacher of salvation," the ego is told. We are called to listen instead to the Holy

Spirit, which offers soul guidance directly from our holy self. It's with the Holy Spirit's help that we learn about forgiveness. Forgiveness is the great undoing that translates perception into knowledge, fear into love, and pain into miracles.

The Course teaches that forgiveness is more than just positive thinking, an emotional reframe, or the overlooking and forgetting of a specific event. Forgiveness is a spiritual path, according to the Course. It is the holy purpose of our life on earth. "Forgiveness is the home of miracles," says the Course. Through forgiveness, we remember who we are. We learn that, in truth, there are no dark nights of the soul, only dark nights of the ego. Forgiveness helps us, therefore, to choose again, to find a better way, and to create a future unlike our past.

"This course is not beyond immediate learning, unless you believe that what God wills takes time," the Course tells us. We can experience a holy shift in our life at any moment and in a single instant. How do we do this? Miracles require no suffering, no sacrifice, no penance, no money, and no special effort. The key is simply "a little willingness" to see what reality is like when you are not lost in fear, guilt, and thoughts of sins. Your little willingness is "powerfully supplemented by the strength of Heaven," says the Course.

The holy shift is our Atonement. "The offer of Atonement is universal," says the Course. "It is equally applicable to all individuals in all circumstances." Miracles are available to everyone who shows a little willingness. "A miracle is *now*. It stands already here, in present grace," says the Course. Therefore, in any holy instant, our weary egos can experience the grace and healing that is on offer from our soul, which is in Heaven and in a state of perfect oneness and wholeness.

My hope is that *Holy Shift!* helps you experience a year of miracles. I've chosen an excerpt from *A Course in Miracles* for each day of the year. I encourage you to set aside time every day—between 1 minute and 15 minutes—to reflect on each message. Each entry is an invitation to a deeper inquiry. Be sure also to take the message with you into your day. *Holy Shift!* is offered as an aid; it is not meant to replace the main work. That said, the main work of *A Course in Miracles* is not to arrive at just an intellectual understanding of the words; it is to identify with the love that brings these words to you. In truth, you *are* this love.

Robert Holden
London, October 2013

A Note to the Reader: Each entry in *Holy Shift!* is taken from either the Text, the Workbook, the Manual for Teachers, or one of the two supplements: Psychotherapy and The Song of Prayer. The references for each entry belong to the 3rd Edition, Combined Volume, of *A Course in Miracles,* published by the Foundation for Inner Peace in 2007. Here is an example of how to read the reference:

Text-18. VIII. 13:1-8.
Chapter 18, Verse 8, paragraph 13, lines 1 to 8.

Workbook-p II. Lesson 360. 1:1-7.
Part II, Lesson 360, paragraph 1, lines 1 to 7.

Manual for Teachers. 14. 5:1-7.
Chapter 14, paragraph 5, lines 1 to 7.

Psychotherapy-3. III. 8:9-13.
Chapter 3, Verse III, paragraph 8, lines 9 to 13.

Song of Prayer-1. I. 1:1-7.
Chapter 1, Verse 1, paragraph 1, lines 1 to 7.

JANUARY

JANUARY 1

*The course does not aim
at teaching the meaning of love,
for that is beyond what can be taught.*

*It does aim, however, at removing the blocks
to the awareness of love's presence,
which is your natural inheritance.*

*The opposite of love is fear, but what is
all-encompassing can have no opposite.*

*This course can therefore be summed up
very simply in this way:*

**Nothing real can be threatened.
Nothing unreal exists.**

Herein lies the peace of God.

Text-Intro. 1:6-8 & 2:1-4.

JANUARY 2

Miracles occur naturally
as expressions
of love.

The real miracle is the
love that inspires
them.

In this sense everything
that comes from love
is a miracle.

Text-1. I.1:1-3.

JANUARY 3

In you is all of Heaven.

Every leaf that falls
is given life
in you.

Each bird that ever sang
will sing again
in you.

And every flower that ever
bloomed has saved
its perfume and
its loveliness
for you.

Text-25. IV. 5:1-4.

JANUARY 4

You are the work of God,
and His work is
wholly lovable
and wholly
loving.

This is how a man
must think of himself
in his heart,
because
this is
what
he
is.

Text-1. III. 2:3-4.

JANUARY 5

Whenever you are
not wholly joyous,
it is because you
have reacted with
a lack of love to
one of God's
creations.

Text-5. VII. 5:1.

JANUARY 6

My holy brother, think of this awhile:
The world you see does nothing.

It has no effects at all.

It merely represents your thoughts.

And it will change entirely as
you elect to change your mind,
and choose the joy of God as
what you really want.

Your Self is radiant in this holy joy,
unchanged, unchanging
and unchangeable,
forever and
forever.

Workbook-p I. Lesson 190. 6:1-5.

JANUARY 7

Dwell not upon the past today.

Keep a completely open mind,
washed of all past ideas and
clean of every concept
you have made.

You have forgiven the world today.
You can look upon it now as if
you never saw it before.

You do not know yet what it
looks like.

You merely wait to have it
shown to you.

While you wait, repeat several times,
slowly and in complete patience:

*The light has come.
I have forgiven the world.*

Workbook-p I. Lesson 75. 6:1-9.

9

JANUARY 8

Salvation requires
the acceptance of but one thought;—
you are as God created you,
not what you made
of yourself.

Whatever evil you may think you did,
you are as God created you.

Whatever mistakes you made,
the truth about you is unchanged.

Creation is eternal and unalterable.
Your sinlessness is guaranteed by God.
You are and will forever be exactly as
you were created.

Light and joy and peace abide in
you because God put
them there.

Workbook-p I. Lesson 93. 7:1-7.

JANUARY 9

It is your thoughts alone that
cause you pain.

Nothing external to your mind
can hurt or injure you in any way.

There is no cause beyond yourself
that can reach down and
bring oppression.

No one but yourself affects you.

There is nothing in the world
that has the power to make you
ill or sad, or weak or frail.

But it is you who have
the power to dominate all things
you see by merely recognizing
what you are.

Workbook-p I. Lesson 190. 5:1-6.

JANUARY 10

I have said you have but two emotions,
love and fear.

One is changeless but continually
exchanged, being offered by the
eternal to the eternal. In this
exchange it is extended, for
it increases as it is given.

The other has many forms, for
the content of individual illusions
differs greatly. Yet they have
one thing in common;
they are all insane.

Text-13. V. 1:1-9.

JANUARY 11

Perception can make
whatever picture
the mind
desires
to see.

Remember this.

In this lies either
Heaven or hell,
as
you
elect.

Manual for Teachers. 19. 5:2-4.

JANUARY 12

Tolerance for pain may be high,
but it is not without limit.

Eventually everyone begins to
recognize, however dimly,
that there *must* be
a better way.

Text-2. III. 3:5-8.

JANUARY 13

The miracle establishes
you dream a dream,
and that its content
is not true.

This is a crucial step in
dealing with illusions.

No one is afraid of them
when he perceives he
made them up.

The fear was held in place
because he did not see
that he was author of
the dream, and not
a figure in the
dream.

Text-28. II. 7:1-4.

JANUARY 14

Forgive us our illusions, Father,
and help us to accept our true relationship
with You, in which there are no illusions,
and where none can ever enter.

Our holiness is Yours.
What can there be in us that needs
forgiveness when Yours is perfect?

The sleep of forgetfulness is only the
unwillingness to remember
Your forgiveness and
Your Love.

Let us not wander into temptation,
for the temptation of the Son of
God is not Your Will.

And let us receive only what You
have given, and accept but this
into the minds which You
created and which
You love.
Amen.

Text-16. VII. 12:1-7.

JANUARY 15

What would you see?
The choice is given you.

But learn and do not let your mind
forget this law of seeing:

You will look upon that which
you feel within.

If hatred finds a place within your heart,
you will perceive a fearful world,
held cruelly in death's
sharp-pointed, bony fingers.

If you feel the Love of God within you,
you will look out on a world
of mercy and of love.

Workbook-pl. Lesson 189. 5:1-5.

JANUARY 16

When the ego was made, God placed
in the mind the Call to joy.

This Call is so strong that the ego
always dissolves at Its sound.

That is why you must choose to hear
one of two voices within you.

One you made yourself, and that
one is not of God.

But the other is given you by God,
Who asks you only to listen to it.

Text-5. II. 3:2-6.

JANUARY 17

What could you not accept, if you
but knew that everything that happens,
all events, past, present and to come,
are gently planned by One Whose
only purpose is your good?

Perhaps you have misunderstood
His plan, for He would never
offer pain to you.

But your defenses did not let you
see His loving blessing shine in
every step you ever took.

While you made plans for death,
He led you gently to
eternal life.

Workbook-p I. Lesson 135. 18:1-4.

JANUARY 18

When you meet anyone,
remember it is a holy
encounter.

As you see him you
will see yourself.

As you treat him you
will treat yourself.

As you think of him you
will think of yourself.

Never forget this, for in him
you will find yourself or
lose yourself.

Text-8. III. 4:1-5.

JANUARY 19

The world but demonstrates an
ancient truth; you will believe
that others do to you exactly
what you think you
did to them.

But once deluded into blaming
them you will not see the
cause of what they do,
because you *want* the
guilt to rest on them.

How childish is the petulant
device to keep your innocence
by pushing guilt outside
yourself, but never
letting go!

Text-27. VIII. 8:1-3.

JANUARY 20

The goal of the curriculum,
regardless of the teacher you choose,
is "Know thyself."

There is nothing else to seek.

Text-8. III. 5:1.

JANUARY 21

Seek not outside yourself.

For all your pain comes simply from
a futile search for what you want,
insisting where it must be found.
What if it is not there?

Do you prefer that you be right or happy?
Be you glad that you are told
where happiness abides,
and seek no longer elsewhere.
You will fail.

But it is given you to know the truth,
and not to seek for it
outside yourself.

Text-29. VII. 1:6-10.

JANUARY 22

You will identify with what you think
will make you safe.

Whatever it may be, you will believe
that it is one with you.

Your safety lies in truth, and not
in lies. Love is your safety.
Fear does not exist.

Identify with love,
and you are
safe.

Identify with love,
and you are
home.

Identify with love,
and find your
Self.

Workbook-p II. Lesson 260. 5. 5:1-8.

JANUARY 23

Simply do this:
Be still, and lay aside
all thoughts of what you are
and what God is;
all concepts you have learned
about the world;
all images you hold
about yourself.

Empty your mind
of everything it thinks is either
true or false, or good or bad,
of every thought it judges worthy,
and all the ideas of which it
is ashamed.

Hold onto nothing.
Do not bring with you
one thought the past has taught,
nor one belief you ever learned
before from anything.

Forget this world,
forget this course,
and come with wholly
empty hands unto
your God.

Workbook-p I. Lesson 189. 7:1-5.

JANUARY 24

Try then, today, to begin
to learn how to look on all things
with love, appreciation and
open-mindedness.

Workbook-p I. Lesson 29. 3:1.

JANUARY 25

When your peace is threatened or disturbed
in any way, say to yourself:

*I do not know what anything, including this,
means. And so I do not know how to
respond to it. And I will not use my
own past learning as the light
to guide me now.*

By this refusal to attempt to teach yourself
what you do not know, the Guide Whom
God has given you will speak to you.

He will take His rightful place in your
awareness the instant you abandon it,
and offer it to Him.

Text-14. XI. 6:6-9.

JANUARY 26

What could you want
forgiveness cannot give?

Do you want peace?
Forgiveness offers it.

Do you want happiness,
a quiet mind, a certainty of purpose,
and a sense of worth and beauty
that transcends the world?

Do you want care and safety,
and the warmth of sure
protection always?

Do you want a quietness that
cannot be disturbed, a gentleness
that never can be hurt, a deep,
abiding comfort, and a rest
so perfect it can never
be upset?

All this forgiveness offers you,
and more.

Workbook-p I. Lesson 122. 1:1-6 to 2:1.

JANUARY 27

Recognizing that what I see reflects
what I think I am, I realize that
vision is my greatest need.

The world I see attests to the fearful
nature of the self-image
I have made.

If I would remember who I am,
it is essential that I let this
image of myself go.

As it is replaced by truth, vision
will surely be given me.

And with this vision, I will
look upon the world and on
myself with charity
and love.

Workbook-p I. Lesson 56. 2:1-7.

JANUARY 28

Seek you no further.

You will not find peace except
the peace of God.

Accept this fact, and save yourself
the agony of yet more
bitter disappointments,
bleak despair, and
sense of icy hopelessness
and doubt.

Seek you no further.

There is nothing else for you to find
except the peace of God, unless
you seek for misery
and pain.

Workbook-p I. Lesson 200. 1:1-5.

JANUARY 29

The journey to God
is merely the reawakening
of the knowledge
of where you are always,
and what you are
forever.

It is a
journey without distance
to a goal
that has
never
changed.

Text-8. VI. 9:6-7.

JANUARY 30

Your
being
is
the
knowledge
of
God.

Text-7. VI. 10:1.

JANUARY 31

You have so little faith in yourself
because you are unwilling to
accept the fact that
perfect love is
in you.

And so you seek without for what
you cannot find without.

I offer you my perfect faith in you,
in place of all your doubts.

But forget not that my faith must be
as perfect in all your brothers as it
is in you, or it would be
a limited gift
to you.

Text-15. VI. 2:1-4.

FEBRUARY

FEBRUARY 1

Projection makes perception.

The world you see is what you gave it,
nothing more than that.

But though it is no more than that,
it is not less.

Therefore, to you it is important.

It is the witness to your state of mind,
the outside picture of an
inward condition.

As a man thinketh, so does
he perceive.

Therefore, seek not to change the
world, but choose to change
your mind about
the world.

Text-21. Intro. 1:1-7.

FEBRUARY 2

Forget not that the healing
of God's Son is all the
world is for.

That is the only purpose the
Holy Spirit sees in it, and
thus the only one
it has.

Until you see the healing of
the Son as all you wish to be
accomplished by the world,
by time and all appearances,
you will not know the Father
nor yourself.

For you will use the world for
what is not its purpose, and
will not escape its laws of
violence and death.

Text-24. VI. 4:1-5.

FEBRUARY 3

Let go of all the trivial things
that churn and bubble on the
surface of your mind, and
reach down and below them
to the Kingdom of Heaven.

There is a place in you where
there is perfect peace.

There is a place in you where
nothing is impossible.

There is a place in you where
the strength of God
abides.

Workbook-p I. Lesson 47. 7:3-6.

FEBRUARY 4

It is hard to understand what
"The Kingdom of Heaven is within you"
really means.

This is because it is not understandable
to the ego, which interprets it as if
something outside is inside, and this
does not mean anything.

The word "within" is unnecessary.

The Kingdom of Heaven
is you.

Text-4. III. 1:1-4.

FEBRUARY 5

The truth in you remains
as radiant as a star,
as pure as light,
as innocent as
love itself.

Text-31. VI. 7:4.

FEBRUARY 6

Your purpose is to see the world
through your own holiness.

Thus are you and the world
blessed together.

No one loses; nothing is taken away
from anyone; everyone gains
through your holy vision.

It signifies the end of sacrifice
because it offers everyone
his full due.

And he is entitled to everything
because it is his birthright as
a Son of God.

Workbook-p I. Lesson 37. 1:2-6.

FEBRUARY 7

Your holiness is totally unlimited
in its power because it establishes you
as a Son of God, at one with the
Mind of his Creator.

Through your holiness
the power of God is made manifest.

Through your holiness
the power of God is made available.

And there is nothing the power
of God cannot do.

Your holiness, then, can remove
all pain, can end all sorrow, and
can solve all problems.

Workbook-p I. Lesson 38. 1:2 & 2:1-4.

FEBRUARY 8

Beyond the body,
beyond the sun and stars, past everything
you see and yet somehow familiar,
is an arc of golden light that
stretches as you look into a
great and shining circle.

And all the circle fills with light before
your eyes. The edges of the circle
disappear, and what is in it is
no longer contained at all.

The light expands and covers everything,
extending to infinity forever shining and
with no break or limit anywhere.

Within it everything is joined in perfect
continuity. Nor is it possible to imagine
that anything could be outside, for
there is nowhere that this
light is not.

This is the vision of the Son of God,
whom you know well.

Text-21. I. 8:1-6 & 9:1.

FEBRUARY 9

You who perceive yourself
as weak and frail,
with futile hopes and
devastated dreams,
born but to die,
to weep and
suffer pain,
hear this:

All power is given
unto you
in earth and
Heaven.

There is nothing
that
you
cannot
do.

Workbook-p I. Lesson 191. 9:1-2.

FEBRUARY 10

Deep within you is everything that is perfect,
ready to radiate through you and out
into the world.

It will cure all sorrow and pain and fear and loss
because it will heal the mind that thought these
things were real, and suffered out of its
allegiance to them.

You can never be deprived of your perfect holiness
because its Source goes with you
wherever you go.

You can never suffer because the Source of all joy
goes with you wherever you go.

You can never be alone because the Source of all life
goes with you wherever you go.

Nothing can destroy your peace of mind because
God goes with you wherever you go.

Workbook-p I. Lesson 41. 3:1-2 & 4:1-4.

FEBRUARY 11

God is indeed your strength,
and what He gives is
truly given.

This means that you can receive
it any time and anywhere,
wherever you are, and in
whatever circumstance
you find yourself.

Your passage through time and
space is not at random.

You cannot but be in the right
place at the right time.

Such is the strength of God.
Such are His gifts.

Workbook-p I. Lesson 42. 2:1-6.

FEBRUARY 12

The sight of Christ
is all there is
to see.

The song of Christ
is all there is
to hear.

The hand of Christ
is all there is
to hold.

There is no journey
but to walk
with Him.

Text-24. V. 7:7-10.

FEBRUARY 13

Christ's vision has one law.
It does not look upon a body, and
mistake it for the Son whom
God created.

It beholds a light beyond the body;
an idea beyond what can be
touched, a purity undimmed by
errors, pitiful mistakes, and
fearful thoughts of guilt from
dreams of sin.

It sees no separation.
And it looks on everyone,
on every circumstance,
all happenings and all events,
without the slightest fading
of the light it sees.

Workbook-p I. Lesson 158. 7:1-5.

FEBRUARY 14

To love yourself is to heal yourself.

Text-11. VIII. 11:3.

FEBRUARY 15

God does not forgive
because He has never condemned.

Workbook-p I. Lesson 46. 1:1.

FEBRUARY 16

God is your safety in every
circumstance.

His Voice speaks for Him in
all situations and in every aspect
of all situations, telling you
exactly what to do to call
upon His strength and
His protection.

There are no exceptions because
God has no exceptions.

And the Voice which speaks
for Him thinks as
He does.

Workbook-p I. Lesson 47. 3:1-4.

FEBRUARY 17

The awareness that
there is nothing to fear
shows that somewhere in your mind,
though not necessarily in a place
you recognize as yet,
you have remembered God,
and let His strength take
the place of your
weakness.

The instant you are willing
to do this there is indeed
nothing to
fear.

Workbook-p I. Lesson 48. 3:2-3.

FEBRUARY 18

It is quite possible to listen to
God's Voice all through the day
without interrupting your regular
activities in any way.

The part of your mind in which
truth abides is in constant
communication with God,
whether you are aware
of it or not.

Workbook-p I. Lesson 49. 1:1-2.

FEBRUARY 19

Put not your faith in illusions.
They will fail you.

Put all your faith in the Love of God
within you; eternal, changeless
and forever unfailing.

This is the answer to whatever
confronts you today.

Through the Love of God within you,
you can resolve all seeming
difficulties without effort and
in sure confidence.

Tell yourself this often today.
It is a declaration of release from
the belief in idols.

It is your acknowledgment of
the truth about yourself.

Workbook-p I. Lesson 50. 4:1-8.

FEBRUARY 20

Remember that
where your heart is,
there
is
your
treasure
also.

Text-2. II. 1:5.

FEBRUARY 21

When I have forgiven myself and
remembered Who I am, I will
bless everyone and
everything I see.

There will be no past,
and therefore no enemies.

And I will look with love on all
that I failed to see
before.

Workbook-p I. Lesson 52. 2:5-7.

FEBRUARY 22

You *will* undertake a journey because you are
not at home in this world.

And you *will* search for your home whether
you realize where it is or not.

If you believe it is outside you the search will
be futile, for you will be seeking it
where it is not.

You do not remember how to look within
for you do not believe your home is there.

Yet the Holy Spirit remembers it for you,
and He will guide you to your home
because that is His mission.

As He fulfills His mission He will teach you
yours, for your mission is the same as His.

By guiding your brothers home
you are but following Him.

Text-12. IV. 5:1-7.

FEBRUARY 23

Sit quietly and close your eyes.
The light within you is sufficient.
It alone has power to give the
gift of sight to you.

Exclude the outer world,
and let your thoughts fly to
the peace within.

They know the way.

For honest thoughts, untainted
by the dream of worldly things
outside yourself, become the
holy messengers of
God Himself.

Workbook-p I. Lesson 188. 6:1-6.

FEBRUARY 24

This is the only thing that you need do for vision,
happiness, release from pain and the complete
escape from sin, all to be given you.

Say only this, but mean it with no reservations,
for here the power of salvation lies:

*I **am** responsible for what I see.*
I choose the feelings I experience, and I
decide upon the goal I would achieve.
And everything that seems to happen to me
I ask for, and receive as I have asked.

Deceive yourself no longer that you are helpless
in the face of what is done to you.

Acknowledge but that you have been mistaken,
and all effects of your mistakes
will disappear.

Text-21. II. 2:1-7.

FEBRUARY 25

Pain, illness, loss, age and death seem
to threaten me.

All my hopes and wishes and plans
appear to be at the mercy of a
world I cannot control.

Yet perfect security and complete
fulfillment are my
inheritance.

I have tried to give my inheritance away
in exchange for the world I see.
But God has kept my
inheritance safe
for me.

My own real thoughts will
teach me what it is.

Workbook-p I. Lesson 56. 1:3-8.

FEBRUARY 26

The miracle comes quietly
into the mind that
stops an instant
and is still.

Text-28. I. 11:1.

FEBRUARY 27

You *are* the Will of God.

Do not accept anything else as your will,
or you are denying what you are.

Deny this and you will attack, believing
you have been attacked. But see the
Love of God in you, and you will see it
everywhere because it *is*
everywhere.

See His abundance in everyone, and
you will know that you are in Him
with them.

They are part of you, as you are part
of God. You are as lonely without
understanding this as God Himself
is lonely when His Sons do
not know Him.

The peace of God is
understanding
this.

Text-7. VII. 10:1-8.

FEBRUARY 28

You always choose between
your weakness and the
strength of Christ
in you.

And what you choose is
what you think
is real.

Text-31. VIII. 2:3-4.

FEBRUARY 29

No course whose purpose is
to teach you to remember
what you really are
could fail to emphasize
that there can never be
a difference in what
you really are
and what
love
is.

Workbook-p I. Lesson 127. 4:1.

MARCH

MARCH 1

Only the Love of God will protect you
in all circumstances.

It will lift you out of every trial,
and raise you high above
all the perceived dangers
of this world into a
climate of perfect peace
and safety.

It will transport you into a state of mind
that nothing can threaten,
nothing can disturb, and
where nothing can intrude
upon the eternal calm of
the Son of God.

Workbook-p I. Lesson 50. 3:1-3.

MARCH 2

You are only love,
but when you deny this,
you make what you are
something you must
learn to remember.

Text-6. III. 2:3.

MARCH 3

Remember that in every attack
you call upon your own weakness,
while each time you forgive
you call upon the strength of
Christ in you.

Do you not then begin to understand
what forgiveness will do for you?

It will remove all sense of weakness,
strain and fatigue from your mind.

It will take away all fear and guilt
and pain.

It will restore the invulnerability
and power God gave His Son
to your awareness.

Workbook-p I. Lesson 62. 3:1-5.

MARCH 4

Forgiveness is the key to happiness.

Here is the answer to your search
for peace.

Here is the key to meaning in a world
that seems to make no sense.

Here is the way to safety in apparent
dangers that appear to threaten you
at every turn, and bring uncertainty
to all your hopes of ever finding
quietness and peace.

Here are all questions answered;
here the end of all uncertainty
ensured at last.

Workbook-p I. Lesson 121. 1:1-4.

MARCH 5

God is not partial.
All His children have His total love,
and all His gifts are freely given to
everyone alike.

Text-1. V. 3:2-3.

MARCH 6

You are sad because
you are not
fulfilling your
function as
co-creator
with God,
and are
therefore
depriving
yourself
of
joy.

Text-7. VI. 13:1.

MARCH 7

*Only you can deprive yourself
of anything.*

Do not oppose this realization,
for it is truly the beginning of
the dawn of light.

Remember also that the denial of
this simple fact takes many forms,
and these you must learn to recognize
and to oppose steadfastly,
without exception.

This is a crucial step in
the reawakening.

Text-11. IV. 4:1-4.

MARCH 8

Love created me like itself.

You need to hear the truth about yourself
as frequently as possible, because
your mind is so preoccupied with
false self-images.

Four or five times an hour, and perhaps
even more, it would be most beneficial
to remind yourself that love created
you like itself.

Hear the truth about yourself
in this.

Workbook-p I. Lesson 67. 5:2-4.

MARCH 9

You who were created
by love like itself can
hold no grievances
and know your
Self.

To hold a grievance
is to forget
who you
are.

Workbook-p I. Lesson 68. 1:1-2.

MARCH 10

Salvation is our only need.

There is no other purpose here,
and no other function
to fulfill.

Learning salvation is our
only goal.

Let us end the ancient search today
by finding the light in us, and
holding it up for everyone who
searches with us to look
upon and rejoice.

Workbook-p I. Lesson 69. 3:2-5.

MARCH 11

Salvation seems to come from
anywhere except from you.

So, too, does the source of guilt.

You see neither guilt nor salvation
as in your own mind and
nowhere else.

When you realize that all guilt is
solely an invention of your
mind, you also realize
that guilt and salvation
must be in the
same place.

In understanding this
you are saved.

Workbook-p I. Lesson 70. 1:2-6.

MARCH 12

[Ask] God to reveal His plan to us.
Ask Him very specifically:

*What would You have
me do?*

*Where would You have
me go?*

*What would You have
me say, and to
whom?*

Workbook-p I. Lesson 71. 9:1-5.

MARCH 13

The light of truth is in us,
where it was placed
by God.

It is the body that is outside us,
and is not our concern.

To be without a body is to be
in our natural state.

To recognize the light of truth
in us is to recognize
ourselves as we are.

To see our Self as separate from
the body is to end the attack on
God's plan for salvation, and
to accept it instead.

And wherever His plan is
accepted, it is
accomplished
already.

Workbook-p I. Lesson 72. 9:1-6.

MARCH 14

Your picture of the world can
only mirror what is within.

The source of neither light nor
darkness can be found
without.

Grievances darken your mind,
and you look out on a
darkened world.

Forgiveness lifts the darkness,
reasserts your will, and lets
you look upon a
world of light.

Workbook-p I. Lesson 73. 5:1-4.

MARCH 15

There is no will but God's.
I seek His peace
today.

Workbook-p I. Lesson 74. 7:2-3.

MARCH 16

The light has come.
You are healed and you can heal.

The light has come.
You are saved and you can save.

You are at peace, and you bring
peace with you wherever you go.
Darkness and turmoil and death
have disappeared.

The light has come.
Today we celebrate the happy ending
to your long dream of disaster.
There are no dark dreams now.

The light has come.
Today the time of light begins for you
and everyone. It is a new era, in
which a new world is born.

The old one has left no trace
upon it in its passing. Today we see
a different world, because
the light has come.

Workbook-p I. Lesson 75. 1:1-7 & 2:1-7.

MARCH 17

The mind that serves the Holy Spirit
is unlimited forever, in all ways,
beyond the laws of time and space,
unbound by any preconceptions,
and with strength and power
to do whatever
it is asked.

Workbook-p I. Lesson 199. 2:1.

MARCH 18

You are entitled to miracles
because of what
you are.

You will receive miracles
because of what
God is.

And you will offer miracles
because you are one
with God.

Again, how simple is salvation!
It is merely a statement of
your true Identity.

It is this that we will
celebrate today.

Workbook-p I. Lesson 77. 1:1-6.

MARCH 19

Perhaps it is not yet quite clear to you
that each decision that you make is
one between a grievance
and a miracle.

Each grievance stands like a dark shield
of hate before the miracle
it would conceal.

And as you raise it up before your eyes,
you will not see the miracle beyond.

Yet all the while it waits for you in light,
but you behold your grievances
instead.

Workbook-p I. Lesson 78. 1:1-4.

MARCH 20

A problem cannot be solved if
you do not know what it is.

Even if it is really solved already
you will still have the problem,
because you will not recognize
that it has been solved.

This is the situation of the world.

The problem of separation,
which is really the only problem,
has already been solved.

Yet the solution is not recognized
because the problem is
not recognized.

Workbook-p I. Lesson 79. 1:1-5.

MARCH 21

A sense of separation from God is
the only lack you really
need correct.

This sense of separation
would never have arisen if you
had not distorted your perception
of truth, and had thus
perceived yourself
as lacking.

Text-1. VI. 2:1-2.

MARCH 22

I am
the light of
the
world.

Forgiveness
is my function
as the light
of the
world.

Workbook-p I. Lesson 81. 1:1 & 3:1.

MARCH 23

My forgiveness is the means by which
the light of the world finds expression
through me.

My forgiveness is the means by which
I become aware of the light of the
world in me.

My forgiveness is the means by which
the world is healed, together with
myself.

Let me, then, forgive the world, that
it may be healed along
with me.

Workbook-p I. Lesson 82. 1:2-5.

MARCH 24

I have no function but the one
God gave me.

This recognition releases me
from all conflict, because it means
I cannot have conflicting goals.

With one purpose only, I am always
certain what to do, what to say
and what to think.

All doubt must disappear as I
acknowledge that my only function
is the one God gave me.

Workbook-p I. Lesson 83. 1:2-5.

MARCH 25

I am in the likeness of
my Creator.

I cannot suffer,
I cannot experience loss
and I cannot die.

I am not a body.

I would recognize my
reality today.

I will worship no idols, nor raise my
own self-concept to replace
my Self.

I am in the likeness of my Creator.

Love created me
like itself.

Workbook-p I. Lesson 84. 1:2-8.

MARCH 26

It is as sure that those who hold grievances
will redefine God in their own image, as it is
certain that God created them like Himself,
and defined them as part of Him.

It is as sure that those who hold grievances
will suffer guilt, as it is certain that those
who forgive will find peace.

It is as sure that those who hold grievances
will forget who they are, as it is certain
that those who forgive will remember.

Workbook-p I. Lesson 68. 3:1-3.

MARCH 27

The emphasis of this course always
remains the same;—it is at this
moment that complete salvation
is offered you, and it is at this
moment that you can
accept it.

This is still your one responsibility.
Atonement might be equated with
total escape from the past and
total lack of interest in
the future.

Heaven is here.
There is nowhere else.
Heaven is now.
There is no other time.

Manual for Teachers. 24. 6:1-7.

MARCH 28

There is no statement that the world is
more afraid to hear than this:

*I do not know the thing I am, and therefore do not
know what I am doing, where I am, or how to look
upon the world or on myself.*

Yet in this learning is salvation born.
And What you are will tell you of Itself.

Text-31. V. 17:6-9.

MARCH 29

You can wait,
delay, paralyze yourself,
or reduce your creativity
almost to nothing.

But you cannot
abolish
it.

Text-1. V. 1:5-6.

MARCH 30

How willing are you to forgive
your brother?

How much do you desire peace
instead of endless strife and
misery and pain?

These questions are the same,
in different form.

Forgiveness is your peace, for herein
lies the end of separation and the
dream of danger and destruction,
sin and death; of madness and
of murder, grief and loss.

This is the "sacrifice" salvation asks,
and gladly offers peace
instead of this.

Text-29. VI. 1:1-5.

MARCH 31

This world is full of miracles.

They stand in shining silence next to
every dream of pain and suffering,
of sin and guilt.

They are the dream's alternative,
the choice to be the dreamer, rather
than deny the active role in
making up the dream.

Text-28. II. 12:1-3.

APRIL

APRIL 1

The miracle is always there.

Its presence is not caused by your vision;
its absence is not the result of
your failure to see.

It is only your awareness of miracles
that is affected.

You will see them in the light;
you will not see them
in the dark.

Workbook-p I. Lesson 91. 1:4-7.

APRIL 2

Miracles honor you because
you are lovable.

They dispel illusions about yourself
and perceive the light in you.

They thus atone for your errors by
freeing you from your
nightmares.

By releasing your mind from the
imprisonment of your illusions,
they restore your
sanity.

Text-1. I. 33:1-4.

APRIL 3

You are what God created or what you made.
One Self is true; the other is not there.
Try to experience the unity
of your one Self.

Try to appreciate Its Holiness and the love
from which It was created.

Try not to interfere with the Self which God
created as you, by hiding Its majesty behind
the tiny idols of evil and sinfulness
you have made to replace It.

Let It come into Its Own.
Here you are; This is You.
And light and joy and peace
abide in you because
this is so.

Workbook-p I. Lesson 93. 9:1-8.

APRIL 4

Today we continue with the one idea
which brings complete salvation;
the one statement which makes all
forms of temptation powerless;
the one thought which renders
the ego silent and entirely undone.

You are as God created you.

The sounds of this world are still,
the sights of this world disappear,
and all the thoughts that this
world ever held are wiped away
forever by this one idea.

Here is salvation accomplished.
Here is sanity restored.

Workbook-p I. Lesson 94. 1:1-5.

APRIL 5

Look upon your brother as yourself.

Your relationship is now a temple of healing;
A place where all the weary ones
can come to rest.

Text-19. III. 11:2-3.

APRIL 6

Salvation
requires the acceptance of but one thought;—
you are as God created you, not
what you made of yourself.

Whatever evil you may think you did,
you are as God created you.

Whatever mistakes you made, the truth
about you is unchanged.

Creation is eternal and unalterable.
Your sinlessness is guaranteed by God.
You are and will forever be exactly as
you were created.

Light and joy and peace abide in you
because God put them there.

Workbook-p I. Lesson 93. 7:1-7.

APRIL 7

Spirit am I,
a holy Son of God,
free of all limits,
safe and
healed
and whole,
free to forgive,
and free to
save
the
world.

Workbook-p I. Lesson 97. 7:2.

APRIL 8

How lovely is the world whose purpose
is forgiveness of God's Son!

How free from fear, how filled with
blessing and with happiness!

And what a joyous thing it is to dwell
a little while in such a happy place!

Nor can it be forgot, in such a world,
it is a little while till timelessness
comes quietly to take the
place of time.

Text-29. VI. 6:1-4.

APRIL 9

You cannot enter into real
relationships with any of God's Sons
unless you love them all
and equally.

Love is not special.

If you single out part of the Sonship
for your love, you are imposing
guilt on all your relationships and
making them unreal.

You can love only as God loves.

Seek not to love unlike him, for
there is no love apart
from His.

Until you recognize that this is true,
you will have no idea what
love is like.

Text-13. X. 11:1-6.

APRIL 10

You are indeed essential to
God's plan.

Just as your light increases every light
that shines in Heaven, so your joy
on earth calls to all minds to let
their sorrows go, and take their
place beside you in
God's plan.

God's messengers are joyous,
and their joy heals sorrow
and despair.

They are the proof that
God wills perfect happiness for all
who will accept their Father's
gifts as theirs.

Workbook-p I. Lesson 100. 4:1-4.

APRIL 11

God's Will for you is perfect happiness
because there is no sin, and
suffering is causeless.

Joy is just, and pain is but the sign
you have misunderstood
yourself.

There is no sin.
Remember this today, and tell yourself
as often as you can:

God's Will for me is perfect happiness.
This is the truth, because
there is no sin.

Workbook-p I. Lesson 101. 6:1-2 & 7:4-7.

APRIL 12

I
share
God's
Will
for
happiness
for
me.

Workbook-p I. Lesson 102.

APRIL 13

No one created by God
can find joy in anything
except the eternal;
not because he is
deprived
of anything else,
but because
nothing else is
worthy
of him.

Text-8. VI. 3:2.

APRIL 14

*I seek but what belongs
to me in truth.*

*God's gifts of joy and peace
are all I want.*

Workbook-p I. Lesson 104. 5:4-5.

APRIL 15

God's peace and joy are yours.

Today we will accept them,
knowing they belong to us.

And we will try to understand
these gifts increase as we
receive them.

They are not like to the gifts the
world can give, in which the
giver loses as he gives the gift;
the taker is the richer by
his loss.

Such are not gifts, but bargains
made with guilt.

The truly given gift entails
no loss.

Workbook-p I. Lesson 105. 1:1-6.

APRIL 16

Prepare yourself for miracles today.

Workbook-p I. Lesson 106. 4:8.

APRIL 17

When a situation
has been dedicated
wholly to truth,
peace is
inevitable.

Text-19. I. 1:1.

APRIL 18

*To give and to receive are
one in truth.*

*I will receive what I am
giving now.*

Workbook-p I. Lesson 108. 8:2-3.

APRIL 19

"I rest in God."
This thought will bring to you the
rest and quiet, peace and stillness,
and the safety and the happiness
you seek.

"I rest in God."
This thought has power to wake
the sleeping truth in you, whose
vision sees beyond appearances
to that same truth in everyone
and everything there is.

Here is the end of suffering for all
the world, and everyone who ever
came and yet will come to
linger for a while.

Here is the thought in which
the Son of God is born again,
to recognize himself.

Workbook-p I. Lesson 109. 2:1-6.

APRIL 20

You are as God created you.

Today honor your Self.

Let graven images you made
to be the Son of God instead of
what he is be worshipped
not today.

Deep in your mind
the holy Christ in you is waiting
your acknowledgment
as you.

And you are lost
and do not know yourself while
He is unacknowledged
and unknown.

Workbook-p I. Lesson 110. 9:1-5.

APRIL 21

In sorting out the false from the true,
the miracle proceeds along
these lines:

Perfect love casts out fear.
If fear exists,
Then there is not perfect love.

But:

Only perfect love exists.
If there is fear,
It produces a state that does
not exist.

Text-1. VI. 5:3-8.

APRIL 22

Pain is illusion; joy, reality.
Pain is but sleep; joy is awakening.
Pain is deception; joy alone is truth.
And so again we make the only choice
that ever can be made: we choose between
illusions and the truth,
or pain and joy
or hell and Heaven.

Workbook-p I. Lesson 190. 10:4-6 & 11:1.

APRIL 23

Hear, then, the one answer of the
Holy Spirit to all the questions
the ego raises:

You are a child of God,
a priceless part of His Kingdom,
which He created as
part of Him.

Nothing else exists and
only this is real.

You have chosen a sleep in which
you have had bad dreams, but the
sleep is not real and God calls
you to awake.

There will be nothing left of your
dream when you hear Him,
because you will awaken.

Text-6. IV. 6:1-4.

APRIL 24

Think not the way to Heaven's gate
is difficult at all.

Nothing you undertake with certain
purpose and high resolve and
happy confidence, holding your
brother's hand and keeping
step to Heaven's song, is
difficult to do.

But it is hard indeed to wander off,
alone and miserable, down a road
that leads to nothing and that
has no purpose.

Text-26. V. 2:4-6.

APRIL 25

It cannot be that it is hard
to do the task that Christ
appointed you to do,
since it is He Who
does it.

Text-25. I. 1:1.

APRIL 26

God's Will is
perfect happiness
for me.

And I can suffer but from
the belief there is
another
will
apart
from
His.

Workbook-p I. Lesson 116. 1:2-3.

APRIL 27

Love wishes to be known,
completely understood
and shared.

It has no secrets;
nothing that it would
keep apart
and hide.

It walks in sunlight,
open-eyed and calm,
in smiling welcome
and in sincerity so simple
and so obvious
it cannot be
misunderstood.

Text-20. VI. 2:5-7.

APRIL 28

The universe of love
does not stop because
you do not see it,
nor have your closed
eyes lost the ability
to see.

Look upon the glory of
His creation, and you
will learn what God
has kept for
you.

Text-11. I. 5:10-11.

APRIL 29

Love will enter immediately into
any mind that truly wants it,
but it must want it truly.

This means that it wants it without
ambivalence, and this kind of
wanting is wholly without
the ego's "drive to get."

Text-4. III. 4:7-8.

APRIL 30

I rest in God today,
and let Him work in me
and through me, while
I rest in Him in quiet
and in perfect
certainty.

Workbook-p I. Lesson 120. 1:2.

MAY

MAY 1

You have no idea of the
tremendous release and deep
peace that comes from meeting
yourself and your brothers
totally without judgment.

When you recognize what you
are and what your brothers are,
you will realize that judging them
in any way is without meaning.

In fact, their meaning is lost to
you precisely *because* you are
judging them.

Text-3. VI. 3:1-3.

MAY 2

You
who
want
peace
can
find it
only
by
complete
forgiveness.

Text-1. VI. 1:1.

MAY 3

Today in gratitude we lift our hearts
above despair, and raise our thankful eyes,
no longer looking downward
to the dust.

We sing the song of thankfulness today,
in honor of the Self that God has willed
to be our true Identity
in Him.

Today we smile on everyone we see,
and walk with lightened footsteps as we
go to do what is appointed us
to do.

Workbook-p I. Lesson 123. 4:1-3.

MAY 4

At one with God
and with the universe
we go our way rejoicing,
with the thought
that God Himself
goes
everywhere
with
us.

Workbook-p I. Lesson 124. 1:5.

MAY 5

In stillness
we will hear God's Voice today
without intrusion of our petty thoughts,
without our personal desires, and
without all judgment of
His holy Word.

We will not judge ourselves today, for
what we are can not be judged.

We stand apart from all the judgments
which the world has laid upon
the Son of God.

It knows him not.

Today we will not listen to the world,
but wait in silence for
the Word of God.

Workbook-p I. Lesson 125. 3:1-5.

MAY 6

Everyone you offer healing
to returns it.

Everyone you attack keeps it
and cherishes it by holding
it against you.

Whether he does this or
does it not will make no
difference; you will think
he does.

It is impossible to offer what
you do not want without
this penalty.

The cost of giving is
receiving.

Text-14. III. 5:4-8.

MAY 7

Perhaps you think that different
kinds of love are possible.

Perhaps you think there is a kind of
love for this, a kind for that;
a way of loving one, another way
of loving still another.

Love is one.

It has no separate parts and no
degrees; no kinds nor levels,
no divergencies and
no distinctions.

It is like itself,
unchanged throughout.

It never alters with a person
or a circumstance.

It is the Heart of God, and
also of His Son.

Workbook-p I. Lesson 127. 1:1-7.

MAY 8

There is a light that this world
cannot give.

Yet you can give it, as it was
given you.

And as you give it, it shines forth
to call you from the world
and follow it.

For this light will attract you as
nothing in this world can do.

And you will lay aside the world
and find another.

This other world is bright with
love which you have given it.

And here will everything remind
you of your Father and
His holy Son.

Text-13. VI. 11:1-7.

MAY 9

Nothing
beyond yourself
can make
you fearful
or loving,
because
nothing
is
beyond
you.

Text-10. Intro. 1:1.

MAY 10

Fear has made everything you think
you see.

All separation, all distinctions,
and the multitude of differences you
believe make up the world.
They are not there.

Love's enemy has made them up.

Yet love can have no enemy, and so
they have no cause, no being
and no consequence.

They can be valued, but remain unreal.
They can be sought, but they can not
be found.

Today we will not seek for them, nor
waste this day in seeking
what can not be found.

Workbook-p I. Lesson 130. 4:1-8.

MAY 11

Why wait for Heaven? It is here today.
Time is the great illusion it is past
or in the future.

Yet this cannot be, if it is where God
wills His Son to be. How could the
Will of God be in the past,
or yet to happen?

What He wills is now, without a past
and wholly futureless.

It is as far removed from time as is
a tiny candle from a distant star,
or what you chose from what
you really want.

Workbook-p I. Lesson 131. 6:1-7.

MAY 12

Perhaps you think you did not make the world,
but came unwillingly to what was
made already, hardly waiting for
your thoughts to give it
meaning.

Yet in truth you found exactly
what you looked for
when you
came.

There is no world apart from
what you wish, and herein
lies your ultimate
release.

Change but your mind on what
you want to see, and all
the world must change
accordingly.

Ideas leave not their
source.

Workbook-p I. Lesson 132. 4:4-5 & 5:1-3.

MAY 13

You do not ask too much of life,
but far too little.

When you let your mind be drawn
to bodily concerns, to things you buy,
to eminence as valued by the world,
you ask for sorrow, not for
happiness.

Workbook-p I. Lesson 133. 2:1-2.

MAY 14

Forgiveness stands between illusions
and the truth; between the world you
see and that which lies beyond;
between the hell of guilt and
Heaven's gate.

Across this bridge, as powerful as love
which laid its blessing on it, are all
dreams of evil and of hatred and
attack brought silently to truth.

They are not kept to swell and bluster,
and to terrify the foolish dreamer
who believes in them.

He has been gently wakened from his
dream by understanding what he
thought he saw was
never there.

Workbook-p I. Lesson 134. 10:4 & 11:1-3.

MAY 15

A healed mind does not plan.
It carries out the plans that it receives
through listening to wisdom
that is not its own.

It waits until it has been taught what
should be done, and then
proceeds to do it.

It does not depend upon itself for
anything except its adequacy
to fulfill the plans
assigned to it.

It is secure in certainty that obstacles
can not impede its progress to
accomplishment of any goal
that serves the greater plan
established for the good
of everyone.

Workbook-p I. Lesson 135. 11:1-5.

MAY 16

Miracles enable you to heal the sick
and raise the dead because you made
sickness and death yourself, and
can therefore abolish both.

You are a miracle,
capable of creating in the likeness
of your Creator.

Everything else is your own
nightmare,
and does not exist.

Only the creations of light
are real.

Text-1. I. 24:1-4.

MAY 17

And as you let yourself be healed,
you see all those around you,
or who cross your mind,
or whom you touch
or those who seem to have no
contact with you, healed
along with you.

Perhaps you will not recognize them all,
nor realize how great your offering
to all the world, when you
let healing come to you.

But you are never healed alone.

And legions upon legions will receive
the gift that you receive when
you are healed.

Workbook-p I. Lesson 137. 10:1-4.

MAY 18

Heaven is the decision I must make.

*I make it now, and will not change
my mind, because it is the
only thing I want.*

Workbook-p I. Lesson 138. 12:5-6.

MAY 19

There is no conflict that does not
entail the single, simple question,
"What am I?"

Workbook-p I. Lesson 139. 1:6.

MAY 20

So do we lay aside
our amulets, our charms
and medicines, our chants and
bits of magic in whatever form
they take.

We will be still and listen for
the Voice of healing, which will cure
all ills as one, restoring saneness to
the Son of God.

No voice but this can cure.

Today we hear a single Voice
which speaks to us of truth,
where all illusions end,
and peace returns to the
eternal, quiet home
of God.

Workbook-p I. Lesson 140. 10:1-4.

MAY 21

My
mind
holds
only
what
I
think
with
God.

Workbook-p I. Lesson 141.

MAY 22

Love is my heritage,
and with it joy.

These are the gifts my Father
gave to me.

I would accept all that is
mine in truth.

Workbook-p I. Lesson 117. 2:2-4.

MAY 23

God indeed can be reached directly,
for there is no distance between
Him and His Son.

His awareness is in everyone's
memory, and His Word is written
on everyone's heart.

Yet this awareness and this memory
can arise across the threshold of
recognition only where all barriers
to truth have been removed.

Manual for Teachers. 26. 1:1-3.

MAY 24

Love's Arms
are open
to receive you,
and
give
you
peace
forever.

Text-20. VI. 10:6.

MAY 25

The question, "What do you want?"
must be answered.

You are answering it every minute and
every second, and each moment of
decision is a judgment that is
anything but ineffectual.

Its effects will follow automatically
until the decision is
changed.

Text-5. V. 6:2-4.

MAY 26

Have faith in only this one thing,
and it will be sufficient:

God wills you be in Heaven,
and nothing can keep you
from it, or it from you.

Your wildest misperceptions,
your weird imaginings, your
blackest nightmares all
mean nothing.

They will not prevail against
the peace God wills
for you.

Text-13. XI. 7:1-3.

MAY 27

There is
no order of difficulty
in miracles.

One is
not "harder" or "bigger"
than another.

They are all the same.

All expressions
of love are
maximal.

Text-1. I. 1:4.

MAY 28

It is not danger that comes when
defenses are laid down.

It is safety.
It is peace.
It is joy.
And it is
God.

Manual for Teachers. 4. VI. 1:11-15.

MAY 29

Those who offer peace to everyone
have found a home in Heaven
the world cannot destroy.

For it is large enough to hold the
world within its peace.

Text-25. IV. 4:9-10.

MAY 30

The song of prayer is silent without
you.

The universe is waiting your release
because it is its own.

Be kind to it and to yourself, and then
be kind to Me. I ask but this;
that you be comforted and live no
more in terror and in pain.

Do not abandon Love.

Remember this; whatever you may
think about yourself, whatever you
may think about the world, your
Father needs you and will call to
you until you come to Him in
peace at last.

Song of Prayer-3. IV. 10:2-7.

MAY 31

Wisdom is not judgment;
it is the relinquishment
of judgment.

Manual for Teachers. 10. 4:5.

JUNE

JUNE 1

No one can suffer loss unless it be
his own decision.

No one suffers pain except his choice
elects this state for him.

No one can grieve nor fear nor think
him sick unless these are the
outcomes that he wants.

And no one dies without his
own consent.

Nothing occurs but represents your wish,
and nothing is omitted that
you choose.

Here is your world, complete
in all details.

Here is its whole reality
for you.

And it is only here
salvation
is.

Workbook-p I. Lesson 152. 1:1-8.

JUNE 2

Today our theme is our defenselessness.
We clothe ourselves in it, as we prepare
to meet the day.

We rise up strong in Christ, and let our
weakness disappear, as we remember
that His strength abides in us.

We will remind ourselves that He remains
beside us through the day, and never
leaves our weakness unsupported by
His strength.

We call upon His strength each time we
feel the threat of our defenses undermine
our certainty of purpose. We will pause a
moment, as He tells us,
"I am here."

Workbook-p I. Lesson 153. 19:1-6.

JUNE 3

Child of God,
you were created to create
the good,
the beautiful,
and the holy.

Do not forget
this.

Text-1. VII. 2:1-2.

JUNE 4

If you knew Who walks beside you
on the way that you have chosen,
fear would be
impossible.

Text-18. III. 3:2.

JUNE 5

"Who walks with me?"

This question should be asked
a thousand times a day, till
certainty has ended doubting
and established peace.

Today let doubting cease.

God speaks for you in answering
your question with these words:

*I walk with God in perfect holiness.
I light the world, I light my mind
and all the minds which God
created one with me.*

Workbook-p I. Lesson 156. 8:1-6.

JUNE 6

Into Christ's Presence will we enter now,
serenely unaware of everything except
His shining face and perfect Love.

The vision of His face will stay with you,
but there will be an instant which
transcends all vision, even this,
the holiest.

This you will never teach,
for you attained it not through
learning.

Yet the vision speaks of your
remembrance of what you
knew that instant, and will
surely know again.

Workbook-p I. Lesson 157. 9:1-4.

JUNE 7

In the ego's language,
"to have" and "to be" are different,
but they are identical to the
Holy Spirit.

The Holy Spirit knows that you both
have everything and
are everything.

Any distinction in this respect
is meaningful only when the idea
of "getting," which implies a lack,
has already been accepted.

This is why
we make no distinction between
having the Kingdom of God and
being the Kingdom of God.

Text-4. III. 9:4-7.

JUNE 8

Christ's vision is a miracle.

It comes from far beyond itself,
for it reflects eternal love and
the rebirth of love which
never dies, but has been
kept obscure.

Christ's vision pictures Heaven,
for it sees a world so like
to Heaven that what God
created perfect can be
mirrored there.

The darkened glass the world
presents can show but twisted
images in broken parts.

The real world pictures
Heaven's innocence.

Workbook-p I. Lesson 159. 3:1-5.

JUNE 9

Not one does Christ forget.

Not one He fails to give you to remember,
that your home may be complete and
perfect as it was established.

He has not forgotten you.

But you will not remember Him
until you look on all as He does.

Who denies his brother is denying Him,
and thus refusing to accept the
gift of sight by which his Self is
clearly recognized, his home
remembered and
salvation
come.

Workbook-p I. Lesson 160. 10:1-5.

JUNE 10

Select one brother, symbol of the rest,
and ask salvation of him.

See him first as clearly as you can, in that same
form to which you are accustomed.

See his face, his hands and feet, his clothing.
Watch him smile, and see familiar gestures
which he makes so frequently.

Then think of this:
What you are seeing now conceals from you
the sight of one who can forgive you all
your sins; whose sacred hands can take
away the nails which pierce your own,
and lift the crown of thorns which
you have placed upon your
bleeding head.

Ask this of him, that he may set you free:

*Give me your blessing, holy Son of God.
I would behold you with the
eyes of Christ, and see my
perfect sinlessness in you.*

Workbook-p I. Lesson 161. 11:1-8.

JUNE 11

*Spirit is in
a state of grace
forever.*

*Your reality
is only
spirit.*

*Therefore
you
are in
a state of grace
forever.*

Text-1. III. 5:4-6.

JUNE 12

Our Father, bless our eyes today.
We are Your messengers, and
we would look upon the glorious
reflection of Your Love which
shines in everything.
We live and move in You alone.
We are not separate from Your
eternal life.
There is no death, for death is
not Your Will.
And we abide where You have
placed us, in the life we share
with You and with all living things,
to be like You and part of
You forever.
We accept Your Thoughts as
ours, and our will is one with
Yours eternally.
Amen.

Workbook-p I. Lesson 163. 9:1-8.

JUNE 13

There is a silence into which
the world can not intrude.

There is an ancient peace you
carry in your heart and
have not lost.

There is a sense of holiness
in you the thought of sin
has never touched.

All this today you will
remember.

Faithfulness in practicing today
will bring rewards so great and
so completely different from
all things you sought before,
that you will know that here
your treasure is, and
here your rest.

Workbook-p I. Lesson 164. 4:1-5.

JUNE 14

The Thought of God created you.

It left you not, nor have you ever been
apart from it an instant.

It belongs to you. By it you live.

It is your Source of life, holding you
one with it, and everything is one
with you because it left you not.

The Thought of God protects you,
cares for you, makes soft your
resting place and smooth your way,
lighting your mind with
happiness and love.

Eternity and everlasting life shine in
your mind, because the
Thought of God has left you not,
and still abides with
you.

Workbook-p I. Lesson 165. 2:1-7.

JUNE 15

All things are given you.

God's trust in you is
limitless.

He knows His Son.
He gives without exception,
holding nothing back that
can contribute to your
happiness.

And yet, unless your will is one
with His, His gifts are not
received.

But what would make you think
there is another will than
His?

Workbook-p I. Lesson 166. 1:1-6.

JUNE 16

There are not different kinds of life,
for life is like the truth. It does
not have degrees.

It is the one condition in which
all that God created share.

Like all His Thoughts, it has no
opposite.

There is no death because what
God created shares His life.

There is no death because an
opposite to God does not exist.

There is no death because the
Father and the Son
are One.

Workbook-p I. Lesson 167. 1:1-7.

JUNE 17

God speaks to us.
Shall we not speak to Him?

He is not distant.
He makes no attempt to hide from us.
We try to hide from Him, and
suffer from deception.

He remains entirely accessible.
He loves His Son.

There is no certainty but this,
yet this suffices.

He will love His Son forever.
When his mind remains asleep,
He loves him still.

And when his mind awakes,
He loves him with a
never-changing
Love.

Workbook-p I. Lesson 168. 1:1-11.

JUNE 18

Grace is acceptance
of the Love of God within
a world of seeming
hate and fear.

By grace alone
the hate and fear are gone,
for grace presents a state so opposite
to everything the world contains,
that those whose minds are lighted
by the gift of grace can not
believe the world of fear
is real.

Workbook-p I. Lesson 169. 2:1-2.

JUNE 19

Today we learn a lesson which can save you
more delay and needless misery than
you can possibly imagine. It is this:

You make what you defend against,
and by your own defense against it is it real
and inescapable. Lay down your arms,
and only then do you perceive it false.

It seems to be the enemy without that you
attack. Yet your defense sets up an enemy
within; an alien thought at war with you,
depriving you of peace, splitting your
mind into two camps which seem
wholly irreconcilable.

For love now has an "enemy," an opposite;
and fear, the alien, now needs your
defense against the threat of
what you really are.

Workbook-p I. Lesson 170. 2:4-7 & 3:1-3.

JUNE 20

God
is
but
Love,
and
therefore
so
am
I.

Workbook-p I. Lesson 171.

JUNE 21

"Teach only love, for that is
what you are."

This is the one lesson that is
perfectly unified, because it is
the only lesson that is one.

Only by teaching it
can you learn it.

"As you teach so will
you learn."

Text-6. III. 2:4-7.

JUNE 22

There is a light in you which cannot die;
whose presence is so holy that the
world is sanctified because
of you.

All things that live bring gifts to you, and
offer them in gratitude and gladness
at your feet.

The scent of flowers is their gift
to you.

The waves bow down before you,
and the trees extend their arms
to shield you from the heat, and lay
their leaves before you on the ground
that you may walk in softness, while
the wind sinks to a whisper round
your holy head.

Workbook-p I. Lesson 156. 4:1-5.

JUNE 23

We have not lost the knowledge
that God gave to us when
He created us like Him.

We can remember it for everyone,
for in creation are all
minds as one.

And in our memory is the recall
how dear our brothers are to us in truth,
how much a part of us is every mind,
how faithful they have really been to us,
and how our Father's Love
contains them all.

Workbook-p I. Lesson 139. 11:4-6.

JUNE 24

When you are afraid,
be still and know that
God is real,
and you are His
Beloved Son in
whom He is
well pleased.

Do not let your ego
dispute this,
because the ego
cannot know what
is as far beyond
its reach as
you are.

Text-4. I. 8:6-7.

JUNE 25

Exempt no one from your love,
or you will be hiding a dark place
in your mind where the Holy Spirit
is not welcome.

And thus you will exempt yourself
from His healing power, for by not
offering total love you will not
be healed.

Text-13. III. 9:2-3.

JUNE 26

In shining peace within you is the
perfect purity in which you
were created.

Fear not to look upon the lovely
truth in you.

Look through the cloud of guilt
that dims your vision, and
look past darkness to the
holy place where you will
see the light.

Text-13. X. 9:4-6.

JUNE 27

Joy has no cost.

It is your sacred right,
and what you pay for
is not happiness.

Text-30. V. 9:9-10.

JUNE 28

You have the right to all the universe;
to perfect peace, complete
deliverance from all effects of sin,
and to the life eternal, joyous and
complete in every way, as God
appointed for His holy Son.

This is the only justice Heaven knows,
and all the Holy Spirit
brings to earth.

Text-25. VIII. 14:1-2.

JUNE 29

What is the Will of God?

He wills His Son have
everything.

And this He guaranteed
when He created him *as*
everything.

It is impossible that
anything be lost, if what
you *have* is what
you *are*.

Text-26. VII. 11:1-4.

JUNE 30

Only appreciation is an
appropriate response
to your brother.

Gratitude is due him
for both his loving thoughts
and his appeals for help,
for both are capable of
bringing love into your
awareness if you
perceive them
truly.

Text-12. I. 6:1-2.

JULY

JULY 1

You are
at home in God,
dreaming of exile but
perfectly capable
of awakening
to reality.

Text-10. I. 2:1.

JULY 2

Whenever you
question your value, say:

God Himself is incomplete without me.

The truth about you is so lofty that
nothing unworthy of God is
worthy of you.

Text-9. VII. 8:1-2, 4.

JULY 3

Father, our Name is Yours.
In It we are united with all living
things, and You Who are their one
Creator. What we made and call
by many different names is but a
shadow we have tried to cast
across Your Own reality. And we
are glad and thankful we
were wrong.

All our mistakes we give to You,
that we may be absolved from all
effects our errors seemed to have.
And we accept the truth You give,
in place of every one of them. Your
Name is our salvation and escape
from what we made. Your Name
unites us in the oneness which is
our inheritance and peace.
Amen.

Workbook-p I. Lesson 184. 15:1-9.

JULY 4

War is the condition in which
fear is born, and grows and
seeks to dominate.

Peace is the state where
love abides, and seeks to
share itself.

Text-23. I. 12:4-5.

JULY 5

The secret of salvation is but this:
that you are doing this unto
yourself.

No matter what the form of the attack,
this still is true.

Whoever takes the role of enemy and
of attacker, still is this the truth.

Whatever seems to be the cause of any
pain and suffering you feel, this is
still true.

For you would not react at all to figures
in a dream you knew that you were
dreaming.

Let them be as hateful and as vicious as
they may, they could have no effect on
you unless you failed to recognize
it is your dream.

Text-27. VIII. 10:1-6.

JULY 6

Never forget you give but
to yourself.

Who understands what giving
means must laugh at the
idea of sacrifice.

Nor can he fail to recognize the
many forms which sacrifice
may take.

He laughs as well at pain and
loss, at sickness and at grief,
at poverty, starvation and
at death.

He recognizes sacrifice remains
the one idea that stands behind
them all, and in his gentle
laughter are they
healed.

Workbook-p I. Lesson 187. 6:1-5.

JULY 7

Why wait for Heaven?
Those who seek the light
are merely
covering
their
eyes.

The light is in them now.

Enlightenment is but
a recognition,
not a
change
at
all.

Workbook-p I. Lesson 188. 1:1-4.

JULY 8

Father, we do not know the way
to You. But we have called, and
You have answered us. We will
not interfere. Salvation's ways
are not our own, for they
belong to You. And it is unto
You we look for them. Our
hands are open to receive
Your gifts. We have no thoughts
we think apart from You, and
cherish no beliefs of what
we are, or Who created us.
Yours is the way that we
would find and follow. And we
ask but that Your Will, which
is our own as well, be done in
us and in the world, that
it become a part of Heaven
now. Amen.

Workbook-p I. Lesson 189. 10:1-10.

JULY 9

Pain is wrong perspective.

When it is experienced in any form,
it is proof of self-deception.

It is not a fact at all.

There is no form it takes that will not
disappear if seen aright.

Workbook-p I. Lesson 190. 1:1-4.

JULY 10

Be glad today how very easily
is hell undone.

You need but tell yourself:

I am the holy Son of God Himself.
I cannot suffer, cannot be in pain;
I cannot suffer loss, nor fail to
do all that salvation asks.

And in that thought is everything
you look on wholly changed.

Workbook-p I. Lesson 191. 7:1-5.

JULY 11

The way is simple.

Every time you feel a stab of anger,
realize you hold a sword above
your head.

And it will fall or be averted as
you choose to be condemned
or free.

Thus does each one who seems to
tempt you to be angry represent
your savior from the prison house
of death.

And so you owe him thanks
instead of pain.

Workbook-p I. Lesson 192. 9:3-7.

JULY 12

This is the lesson God would have
you learn:

There is a way to look on everything
that lets it be to you another step
to Him, and to salvation of
the world.

To all that speaks of terror,
answer thus:

I will forgive, and this will disappear.

To every apprehension, every care and
every form of suffering, repeat these
selfsame words.

And then you hold the key that opens
Heaven's gate, and brings the
Love of God the Father down to earth
at last, to raise it up
to Heaven.

Workbook-p I. Lesson 193. 13:1-5.

JULY 13

I
place
the
future
in
the
Hands
of
God.

Workbook-p I. Lesson 194.

JULY 14

Today we learn to think of gratitude in
place of anger, malice and
revenge.

We have been given everything.

If we refuse to recognize it, we are not
entitled therefore to our bitterness,
and to a self-perception which regards
us in a place of merciless pursuit,
where we are badgered ceaselessly,
and pushed about without a thought or
care for us or for our future.

Gratitude becomes the single thought
we substitute for these
insane perceptions.

Workbook-p I. Lesson 195. 9:1-4.

JULY 15

It can be but myself I crucify.

When this is firmly understood
and kept in full awareness,
you will not attempt to
harm yourself, nor make
your body slave to
vengeance.

You will not attack yourself,
and you will realize that
to attack another is but
to attack yourself.

You will be free
of the insane belief that
to attack a brother
saves yourself.

And you will understand
his safety is your own, and
in his healing you
are healed.

Workbook-p I. Lesson 196. 1:1-4.

JULY 16

What is Heaven but a
song of gratitude and love
and praise by everything
created to the Source
of its creation?

The holiest of altars is set
where once sin was
believed to be.

And here does every light of
Heaven come, to be
rekindled and increased
in joy.

For here is what was lost
restored to them, and
all their radiance made
whole again.

Text-26. IV. 3:5-8.

JULY 17

Today we practice letting freedom
come to make its home with you.

The truth bestows these words upon
your mind, that you may find the key
to light and let the darkness end:

Only my condemnation injures me.
Only my own forgiveness sets me free.

Do not forget today that there can be
no form of suffering that fails to hide
an unforgiving thought.

Nor can there be a form of pain
forgiveness cannot heal.

Workbook-p I. Lesson 198. 9:1-6.

JULY 18

And God Himself extends His Love
and happiness each time you say:

I am not a body. I am free.
I hear the Voice that God has given me,
and it is only this my mind obeys.

Workbook-p I. Lesson 199. 8:6-9.

JULY 19

No one who truly seeks
the peace of God
can fail to
find it.

Workbook-p I. Lesson 185. 11:1.

JULY 20

I am not a body.

I am free.

For I am still
as
God
created
me.

Workbook-p I. Lesson 201.

JULY 21

There is one thing that you have never
done; you have not utterly forgotten
the body.

It has perhaps faded at times from
your sight, but it has not yet
completely disappeared.

You are not asked to let this happen
for more than an instant, yet it is in
this instant that the miracle of
Atonement happens.

Afterwards you will see the body again,
but never quite the same.

And every instant that you spend
without awareness of it gives you a
different view of it when
you return.

Text-18. VII. 2:1-5.

JULY 22

Who hangs an empty frame upon a wall
and stands before it, deep in reverence,
as if a masterpiece were there
to see?

Yet if you see your brother as a body,
it is but this you do.

The masterpiece that God has set within
this frame is all there is to see.

The body holds it for a while, without
obscuring it in any way.

Yet what God has created needs no
frame, for what He has created He
supports and frames within Himself.

His masterpiece He offers you to see.
And would you rather see the frame
instead of this? And see the
picture not at all?

Text-25. II. 5:1-8.

JULY 23

Your mission is very simple.

You are asked to live
so as to demonstrate that
you are
not
an
ego.

Text-4. VI. 6:2-3.

JULY 24

You
believe
that without the ego,
all would be
chaos.

Yet
I assure you
that without the ego,
all would be
love.

Text-15. V. 1:6-7.

JULY 25

When I said
"I am with you always,"
I meant it literally.

I am not absent to anyone
in any situation.

Because I am always with you,
you are the way,
the truth and
the life.

Text-7. III. 1:7-9.

JULY 26

God's blessing shines upon me
from within my heart,
where He abides.

I need but turn to Him,
and every sorrow melts away,
as I accept His boundless
Love for me.

Workbook-p I. Lesson 207. 1:2-3.

JULY 27

*I will be still,
and let the earth be still
along with me.*

*And in that stillness
we will find the
peace of God.*

*It is within my heart,
which witnesses to
God Himself.*

Workbook-p I. Lesson 208. 1:2-4.

JULY 28

*The Love of God is
what created
me.*

*The Love of God is
everything
I am.*

*The Love of God
proclaimed me as
His Son.*

*The Love of God
within me sets
me free.*

Workbook-p I. Lesson 209. 1:2-5.

JULY 29

Remember the sorrowful story
of the world, and the glad
tidings of salvation.

Remember the plan of God for
the restoration of joy and
peace.

And do not forget how very
simple are the ways of God:

*You were lost in the darkness of
the world until you asked for light.
And then God sent His Son
to give it to you.*

Psychotherapy-3. III. 8:9-13.

JULY 30

When God gave Himself to you
in your creation, He
established you as host to
Him forever.

He has not left you, and you
have not left Him.

All your attempts to deny His
magnitude, and make His Son
hostage to the ego, cannot
make little whom God
has joined with Him.

Every decision you make is
for Heaven or for hell, and
brings you the awareness
of what you decided for.

Text-15. III. 5:4-7.

JULY 31

Would you be hostage to the ego
or host to God?

You will accept only whom you
invite.

You are free to determine who shall
be your guest, and how long he
shall remain with you.

Yet this is not real freedom, for it still
depends on how you see it.

The Holy Spirit is there, although He
cannot help you without your invitation.

And the ego is nothing, whether you
invite it in or not.

Real freedom depends on welcoming
reality, and of your guests only the
Holy Spirit is real.

Text-11. II. 7:1-7.

AUGUST

AUGUST 1

Trials are but lessons that
you failed to learn presented once again,
so where you made a faulty choice before
you now can make a better one, and thus
escape all pain that what you chose
before has brought to you.

In every difficulty, all distress,
and each perplexity Christ calls to you
and gently says, "My brother,
choose again."

Text-31. VIII. 3:1-2.

AUGUST 2

The Holy Spirit will always guide you truly,
because your joy is His.

This is His Will for everyone because He
speaks for the Kingdom of God, which
is joy.

Following Him is therefore the easiest thing
in the world, and the only thing that is easy,
because it is not of the world.

It is therefore natural.

Text-7. XI. 1:1-4.

AUGUST 3

*The Holy Spirit is
my only
Guide.*

*He walks with me
in
love.*

*And I give thanks to Him
for showing me
the way
to
go.*

Workbook-p I. Lesson 215. 1:2-4.

AUGUST 4

All that I do
I do
unto
myself.

If I attack,
I suffer.

But if I forgive,
salvation
will
be
given
me.

Workbook-p I. Lesson 216. 1:2-4.

AUGUST 5

Let us be glad that we can walk the world,
and find so many chances to perceive
another situation where God's gift can
once again be recognized as ours!

And thus will all the vestiges of hell, the
secret sins and hidden hates be gone.

And all the loveliness which they
concealed appear like lawns of Heaven
to our sight, to lift us high above the
thorny roads we travelled on before
the Christ appeared.

Text-31. VIII. 9:1-3.

AUGUST 6

The holiest of all the spots on
earth is where an ancient hatred
has become a present love.

Text-26. IX. 6:1.

AUGUST 7

Temptation has one lesson it would teach,
in all its forms, wherever it occurs.

It would persuade the holy Son of God he
is a body, born in what must die, unable
to escape its frailty, and bound by what
it orders him to feel.

It sets the limits on what he can do;
its power is the only strength he has;
his grasp cannot exceed its tiny reach.

Would you be this, if Christ appeared to
you in all His glory, asking you but this:

Choose once again if you would take your
place among the saviors of the world,
or would remain in hell, and hold your
brothers there.

Text-31. VIII. 1:1-5.

AUGUST 8

Let me not wander
from the way of peace,
for I am lost on
other roads
than this.

But let me follow Him
Who leads me home,
and peace is certain
as the Love
of God.

Workbook-p I. Lesson 220. 1:2-3.

AUGUST 9

Father, I come to You today
to seek the peace that
You alone can give.

I come in silence.
In the quiet of my heart,
the deep recesses of my mind,
I wait and listen for Your Voice.

My Father, speak to me today.
I come to hear Your Voice
in silence and in certainty and love,
sure You will hear my call
and answer me.

Workbook-p II. Lesson 221. 1:1-5.

AUGUST 10

God is with me.

He is my Source of life,
the life within, the air I breathe,
the food by which I am sustained,
the water which renews
and cleanses me.

He is my home,
wherein I live and move;
the Spirit which directs my actions,
offers me Its Thoughts,
and guarantees my safety
from all pain.

He covers me with kindness
and with care, and holds in love
the Son He shines upon, who
also shines on Him.

How still is he who knows
the truth of what He speaks
today!

Workbook-p II. Lesson 222. 1:1-5.

AUGUST 11

I was mistaken when I thought
I lived apart from God, a separate entity
that moved in isolation, unattached,
and housed within a body.

Now I know my life is God's,
I have no other home, and I do
not exist apart from Him.

He has no Thoughts that are not
part of me, and I have none but
those which are of Him.

Workbook-p II. Lesson 223. 1:1-3.

AUGUST 12

My true Identity is so secure,
so lofty, sinless, glorious and great,
wholly beneficent and free from guilt,
that Heaven looks to It
to give it light.

It lights the world as well.

It is the gift my Father gave to me;
the one as well I give the world.

There is no gift but this that can
be either given or received.

This is reality, and only this.
This is illusion's end.
It is the truth.

Workbook-p II. Lesson 224. 1:1-7.

AUGUST 13

Prayer is the greatest gift with which
God blessed His Son at his creation.

It was then what it is to become;
the single voice Creator and creation share;
the song the Son sings to the Father,
Who returns the thanks it offers Him
unto the Son.

Endless the harmony, and endless, too,
the joyous concord of the Love They
give forever to Each Other.

And in this, creation is extended.

Song of Prayer-1. Intro. 1:1-4.

AUGUST 14

Prayer is a ladder reaching up
to Heaven.

At the top there is a transformation
much like your own, for prayer is
part of you.

The things of earth are left behind,
all unremembered.

There is no asking, for there is
no lack.

Identity in Christ is fully recognized
as set forever, beyond all change
and incorruptible.

The light no longer flickers, and will
never go out.

Song of Prayer-1. II. 7:1-6.

AUGUST 15

Father, it is today that I am free,
because my will is Yours. I
thought to make another will.
Yet nothing that I thought apart
from You exists. And I am free
because I was mistaken, and
did not affect my own reality at all
by my illusions. Now I give them
up, and lay them down before
the feet of truth, to be removed
forever from my mind. This is
my holy instant of release.
Father, I know my will is one
with Yours.

Workbook-p II. Lesson 227. 1:1-7.

AUGUST 16

God has condemned
me not.

No more do I.

Workbook-p II. Lesson 228. 2:1-6.

AUGUST 17

I seek my own Identity,
and find It in these words:

"Love, which created me,
is what I am."

Now need I seek no more.

Love has prevailed.

So still It waited for my coming home,
that I will turn away no longer from
the holy face of Christ.

And what I look upon attests
the truth of the Identity I sought
to lose, but which my Father
has kept safe for
me.

Workbook-p II. Lesson 229. 1:1-5.

AUGUST 18

Father, I seek the peace You
gave as mine in my creation.
What was given then must be
here now, for my creation was
apart from time, and still
remains beyond all change.
The peace in which Your Son
was born into Your Mind is
shining there unchanged.
I am as You created me.
I need but call on You to find
the peace You gave.
It is Your Will that gave it
to Your Son.

Workbook-p II. Lesson 230. 2:1-6.

AUGUST 19

*What can I seek for, Father, but
Your Love? Perhaps I think I
seek for something else; a
something I have called by many
names. Yet is Your Love the only
thing I seek, or ever sought. For
there is nothing else that I could
ever really want to find. Let me
remember You. What else could
I desire but the truth about
myself?*

Workbook-p II. Lesson 231. 1:1-6.

AUGUST 20

*Be in my mind, my Father, when
I wake, and shine on me
throughout the day today. Let
every minute be a time in which
I dwell with You. And let me not
forget my hourly thanksgiving
that You have remained with me,
and always will be there to hear
my call to You and answer me.
As evening comes, let all my
thoughts be still of You and of
Your Love. And let me sleep sure
of my safety, certain of Your
care, and happily aware I am
Your Son.*

Workbook-p II. Lesson 232. 1:1-5.

AUGUST 21

*Father, I give You all my
thoughts today. I would have
none of mine. In place of them,
give me Your Own. I give You
all my acts as well, that I may
do Your Will instead of seeking
goals which cannot be obtained,
and wasting time in vain
imaginings. Today I come to
You. I will step back and merely
follow You. Be You the Guide,
and I the follower who questions
not the wisdom of the Infinite,
nor Love whose tenderness I
cannot comprehend, but which
is yet Your perfect gift
to me.*

Workbook-p II. Lesson 233. 1:1-7.

AUGUST 22

Today we will anticipate
the time when dreams of sin
and guilt are gone, and we
have reached the holy peace
we never left.

Merely a tiny instant
has elapsed between eternity
and timelessness.

So brief the interval there was no
lapse in continuity, nor break in
thoughts which are forever
unified as one.

Nothing has ever happened
to disturb the peace of
God the Father and
the Son.

This we accept as wholly
true today.

Workbook-p II. Lesson 234. 1:1-5.

AUGUST 23

Father,
Your Holiness is mine.

Your Love created me,
and made my sinlessness forever
part of You.

I have no guilt nor sin in me,
for there is none
in You.

Workbook-p II. Lesson 235. 2:1-3.

AUGUST 24

Father,
my mind is open
to Your Thoughts,
and closed today
to every thought
but Yours.

I rule my mind,
and offer it
to You.

Accept my gift,
for it is Yours
to me.

Workbook-p II. Lesson 236. 2:1-3.

AUGUST 25

You need to
learn to lay all fear aside,
and know your Self
as Love which
has no
opposite
in
you.

Workbook-p I. Lesson 99. 9:8.

AUGUST 26

When you have learned how
to decide with God, all decisions
become as easy and as
right as breathing.

There is no effort, and you will
be led gently as if you were
being carried down a
quiet path in
summer.

Text-14. IV. 6:1-2.

AUGUST 27

We thank You, Father,
for the light that shines
forever in us. And
we honor it, because
You share it with us.
We are one, united in
this light and one with
You, at peace with
all creation and
ourselves.

Workbook-p II. Lesson 239. 2:1-3.

AUGUST 28

Let us not be deceived
today.

We are the Sons of God.

There is no fear in us, for
we are each a part
of Love Itself.

Workbook-p II. Lesson 240. 1:6-8.

AUGUST 29

Forgiveness recognizes what you
thought your brother did to you
has not occurred.

It does not pardon sins and make
them real. It sees there was no sin.

And in that view are all your
sins forgiven.

What is sin, except a false idea
about God's Son?

Forgiveness merely sees its falsity,
and therefore lets it go.

What then is free to take its place is
now the Will of God.

Workbook-p II. 1. 1:1-7.

AUGUST 30

I will not lead my life alone
today.

I do not understand the world,
and so to try to lead my life alone
must be but foolishness.

But there is One Who knows all
that is best for me. And He is glad
to make no choices for me but
the ones that lead to God.

I give this day to Him, for I would
not delay my coming home, and
it is He Who knows the way
to God.

Workbook-p II. Lesson 242. 1:1-5.

AUGUST 31

A dream of judgment came into
the mind that God created
perfect as Himself.

And in that dream was Heaven
changed to hell, and God
made enemy unto
His Son.

How can God's Son awaken
from the dream?

It is a dream of judgment.
So must he judge not, and
he will waken.

Text-29. IX. 2:1-5.

SEPTEMBER

SEPTEMBER 1

The Holy Spirit always sides with you
and with your strength.

As long as you avoid His guidance
in any way, you want
to be weak.

Text-7. X. 5:1-2.

SEPTEMBER 2

Your peace surrounds me,
Father. Where I go, Your peace
goes there with me. It sheds its
light on everyone I meet. I bring
it to the desolate and lonely and
afraid. I give Your peace to
those who suffer pain, or grieve
for loss, or think they are bereft
of hope and happiness.
Send them to me, my Father.
Let me bring Your peace with me.
For I would save Your Son, as
is Your Will, that I may come
to recognize my Self.

Workbook-p II. Lesson 245. 1:1-8.

SEPTEMBER 3

Let me not think that
I can find the way to God,
if I have hatred in
my heart.

Let me not try to hurt
God's Son, and think that I
can know his Father
or my Self.

Let me not fail to recognize
myself, and still believe that my
awareness can contain my Father,
or my mind conceive of all the
love my Father has for me,
and all the love which
I return to Him.

Workbook-p II. Lesson 246. 1:1-3.

SEPTEMBER 4

And all that stood between
your image of yourself
and what you are,
forgiveness
washes
joyfully
away.

Text-30. V. 6:2.

SEPTEMBER 5

Whatever suffers is not part of me.

What grieves is not myself.

What is in pain is but illusion
in my mind.

What dies was never living in reality,
and did but mock the truth
about myself.

Now I disown self-concepts and
deceits and lies about the
holy Son of God.

Now am I ready to accept him back
as God created him, and
as he is.

Workbook-p II. Lesson 248. 1:3-8.

SEPTEMBER 6

Forgiveness
paints a picture of a world
where suffering is over,
loss becomes impossible
and anger makes
no sense.

Attack is gone,
and madness has an end.
What suffering is now conceivable?
What loss can be sustained?

The world becomes a place of joy,
abundance, charity and
endless giving.

It is now so like to Heaven
that it quickly is transformed
into the light that
it reflects.

And so the journey
which the Son of God began
has ended in the light
from which he
came.

Workbook-p II. Lesson 249. 1:1-7.

SEPTEMBER 7

Who would attempt to fly
with the tiny wings of a sparrow
when the mighty power of an eagle
has been given him?

And who would place his faith
in the shabby offerings of the ego
when the gifts of God are laid
before him?

Manual for Teachers. 4. I. 2:2-3.

SEPTEMBER 8

All that I sought before I needed not,
and did not even want.

My only need I did not recognize.
But now I see that I need
only truth.

In that all needs are satisfied,
all cravings end, all hopes
are finally fulfilled and
dreams are gone.

Now have I everything that I
could need.

Now have I everything that I
could want.

And now at last I find myself
at peace.

Workbook-p II. Lesson 251. 1:3-9.

SEPTEMBER 9

My Self is holy beyond all the thoughts
of holiness of which I now conceive.

Its shimmering and perfect purity is far
more brilliant than is any light that I have
ever looked upon.

Its love is limitless, with an intensity
that holds all things within it, in the
calm of quiet certainty.

Its strength comes not from burning
impulses which move the world, but
from the boundless Love of God
Himself.

How far beyond this world my Self
must be, and yet how near
to me and close to God!

Workbook-p II. Lesson 252. 1:1-5.

SEPTEMBER 10

"Except ye become as little children"
means that unless you fully
recognize your complete dependence
on God, you cannot know
the real power of the Son
in his true relationship with
the Father.

Text-1. V. 3:4.

SEPTEMBER 11

Let every
voice but God's
be still
in
me.

Workbook-p II. Lesson 254.

SEPTEMBER 12

In His Name,
I give today to finding what
my Father wills for me,
accepting it as mine,
and giving it to all my
Father's Sons,
along with
me.

Workbook-p II. Lesson 255. 1:6.

SEPTEMBER 13

God is our goal; forgiveness is
the means by which our minds
return to Him at last.

*And so, our Father, would we
come to You in Your appointed
way. We have no goal except to
hear Your Voice, and find the
way Your sacred Word has
pointed out to us.*

Workbook-p II. Lesson 256. 1:9 & 2:1-2.

SEPTEMBER 14

Let
me
remember
what
my
purpose
is.

Workbook-p II. Lesson 257.

SEPTEMBER 15

All that is needful is to train our minds
to overlook all little senseless aims,
and to remember that
our goal is God.

His memory is hidden in our minds,
obscured but by our pointless
little goals which offer nothing,
and do not exist.

Shall we continue to allow God's grace
to shine in unawareness, while the
toys and trinkets of the world
are sought instead?

God is our only goal, our only Love.
We have no aim but to
remember Him.

Workbook-p II. Lesson 258. 1:1-5.

SEPTEMBER 16

We are free to
choose our joy instead of pain,
our holiness in place of sin,
the peace of God instead of conflict,
and the light of Heaven for
the darkness of the
world.

Workbook-p I. Lesson 190. 11:2.

SEPTEMBER 17

You do not walk alone.

God's angels hover near
and all about.

His Love surrounds you,
and of this be sure;
that I will never leave you
comfortless.

Workbook-p II. Epilogue. 6:6-8.

SEPTEMBER 18

I live in God.

In Him I find my refuge
and my strength.

In Him is my Identity.

In Him is everlasting peace.

And only there will I remember
Who I really am.

Workbook-p II. Lesson 261. 1:4-8.

SEPTEMBER 19

Father, You have one Son. And it is
he that I would look upon today.
He is Your one creation.
Why should I perceive a thousand
forms in what remains as one?
Why should I give this one a thousand
names, when only one suffices?
For Your Son must bear Your Name,
for You created him.
Let me not see him as stranger to
his Father, nor as stranger to myself.
For he is part of me and I of him, and
we are part of You Who are our
Source, eternally united in Your Love;
eternally the holy Son of God.

Workbook-p II. Lesson 262. 1:1-8.

SEPTEMBER 20

There is no miracle you cannot have
when you desire healing.

But there is no miracle that can be
given you unless you
want it.

Text-30. VIII. 4:5-6.

SEPTEMBER 21

I
am
surrounded
by the
Love
of
God.

Workbook-p II. Lesson 264.

SEPTEMBER 22

In quietness are all things
answered, and is every
problem quietly
resolved.

Text-27. IV. 1:1.

SEPTEMBER 23

I am here only to be truly helpful.
I am here to represent Him Who sent me.
I do not have to worry about what to say or what
to do, because He Who sent me will direct me.
I am content to be wherever He wishes, knowing
He goes there with me.
I will be healed as I let Him teach me to heal.

Text-2. V. 18:2-6.

SEPTEMBER 24

My
heart
is
beating
in
the
peace
of
God.

Workbook-p II. Lesson 267.

SEPTEMBER 25

*In love
was I created, and
in love
will I remain
forever.*

*What can frighten me,
when I let all things
be exactly as
they are?*

Workbook-p II. Lesson 268. 1:5-6.

SEPTEMBER 26

Today I choose to see
a world forgiven, in which
everyone shows me the
face of Christ, and
teaches me that what I look
upon belongs to me;
that nothing is, except
Your holy Son.

Workbook-p II. Lesson 269. 1:5.

SEPTEMBER 27

Christ is our eyes today.

And through His sight we
offer healing to the world
through Him, the holy
Son whom God created
whole; the holy Son
whom God created
One.

Workbook-p II. Lesson 270. 2:2-3.

SEPTEMBER 28

Each day, each hour, every instant,
I am choosing what I want to look upon,
the sounds I want to hear,
the witnesses to what I want
to be the truth
for me.

Today I choose to look upon what
Christ would have me see,
to listen to God's Voice,
and seek the witnesses to
what is true in God's
creation.

Workbook-p II. Lesson 271. 1:1-2.

SEPTEMBER 29

Father, the truth belongs to me.
My home is set in Heaven by
Your Will and mine.
Can dreams content me?
Can illusions bring me happiness?
What but Your memory can
satisfy Your Son?
I will accept no less than You
have given me.
I am surrounded by Your Love,
forever still, forever gentle and
forever safe.
God's Son must be as
You created him.

Workbook-p II. Lesson 272. 1:1-8.

SEPTEMBER 30

Father, Your peace is mine.
What need have I to fear that
anything can rob me of what
You would have me keep?
I cannot lose Your gifts to me.
And so the peace You gave
Your Son is with me still,
in quietness and in my own
eternal love for You.

Workbook-p II. Lesson 273. 2:1-4.

OCTOBER

OCTOBER 1

Today
belongs
to
love.

Let
me
not
fear.

Workbook-p II. Lesson 274.

OCTOBER 2

There are many answers
you have already received
but have not yet
heard.

I assure you that they are
waiting for you.

Text-9. II. 3:6-7.

OCTOBER 3

What is the Word of God?

"My Son is pure and holy
as Myself."

Workbook-p II. Lesson 276. 1:1-2.

OCTOBER 4

Every loving thought is true.

Everything else is an appeal for
healing and help, regardless
of the form it takes.

Text-12. I. 3:3-4.

OCTOBER 5

Whenever you deny
a blessing to a brother
you will feel deprived,
because denial is
as total as
love.

Text-7. VII. 1:1.

OCTOBER 6

The end of dreams is promised me,
because God's Son is not abandoned
by His Love.

Only in dreams is there a time when he
appears to be in prison, and awaits a
future freedom, if it be at all.

Yet in reality his dreams are gone,
with truth established in their place.

And now is freedom his already.
Should I wait in chains which have
been severed for release,
when God is offering me
freedom now?

Workbook-p II. Lesson 279. 1:1-5.

OCTOBER 7

It is impossible for a child of God
to love his neighbor except
as himself.

That is why the healer's prayer is:

*Let me know this brother as
I know myself.*

Text-5. Intro. 3:6-8.

OCTOBER 8

Father, Your Son is perfect.
When I think that I am hurt in any
way, it is because I have forgotten
who I am, and that I am as You
created me. Your Thoughts can
only bring me happiness. If ever
I am sad or hurt or ill, I have
forgotten what You think, and put
my little meaningless ideas in
place of where Your Thoughts
belong, and where they are.
I can be hurt by nothing but my
thoughts. The Thoughts I think
with You can only bless.
The Thoughts I think with You
alone are true.

Workbook-p II. Lesson 281. 1:1-7.

OCTOBER 9

All healing
is
essentially
the
release
from
fear.

Text-2. IV. 1:7.

OCTOBER 10

*Father, I made an image of
myself, and it is this I call the
Son of God. Yet is creation as it
always was, for Your creation is
unchangeable. Let me not
worship idols. I am he my
Father loves. My holiness
remains the light of Heaven and
the Love of God. Is not what is
beloved of You secure? Is not
the light of Heaven infinite?
Is not Your Son my true Identity,
when You created everything
that is?*

Workbook-p II. Lesson 283. 1:1-8.

OCTOBER 11

Comparison
must be an ego device,
for
love
makes
none.

Text-24. II. 1:1.

OCTOBER 12

Today I wake with joy,
expecting but the
happy things of God
to come
to me.

Workbook-p II. Lesson 285. 1:1.

OCTOBER 13

Father, how still today!
How quietly do all things fall in place!
This is the day that has been chosen as
the time in which I come to understand the
lesson that there is no need that I do anything.
In You is every choice already made.
In You has every conflict been resolved.
In You is everything I hope to find
already given me. Your peace is mine.
My heart is quiet, and my mind at rest.
Your Love is Heaven, and
Your Love is mine.

Workbook-p II. Lesson 286. 1:1-9.

OCTOBER 14

In any situation in which you are uncertain,
the first thing to consider, very simply, is
"What do I want to come of this?
What is it *for?*"

The clarification of the goal belongs at the
beginning, for it is this which will
determine the outcome.

Text-17. IV. 2:1-3.

OCTOBER 15

All
healing
is
release
from
the
past.

Text-13. VIII. 1:1.

OCTOBER 16

Unless the past is over in my mind,
the real world must escape
my sight.

For I am really looking nowhere;
seeing but what is not there.

How can I then perceive the world
forgiveness offers? This the past was
made to hide, for this the world
that can be looked on
only now.

It has no past.

For what can be forgiven but
the past, and if it is forgiven
it is gone.

Workbook-p II. Lesson 289. 1:1-6.

OCTOBER 17

Unless I look upon what is not there,
my present happiness is all I see.

Eyes that begin to open see at last.
And I would have Christ's vision come
to me this very day.

What I perceive without God's Own Correction
for the sight I made is frightening
and painful to behold.

Yet I would not allow my mind to be
deceived by the belief the dream I made
is real an instant longer.

This the day I seek my present happiness,
and look on nothing else except
the thing I seek.

Workbook-p II. Lesson 290. 1:1-6.

OCTOBER 18

Christ's vision looks through me today.

His sight shows me all things forgiven
and at peace, and offers this same
vision to the world.

And I accept this vision in its name,
both for myself and for the
world as well.

What loveliness we look upon today!
What holiness we see surrounding us!
And it is given us to recognize it is a
holiness in which we share;
it is the Holiness of
God Himself.

Workbook-p II. Lesson 291. 1:1-6.

OCTOBER 19

It takes
great learning
to understand that
all things, events,
encounters and
circumstances
are helpful.

Manual for Teachers. 4. 1A. 4:5.

OCTOBER 20

All fear is past, because its source
is gone, and all its thoughts
gone with it.

Love remains the only present state,
whose Source is here forever
and forever.

Can the world seem bright and clear
and safe and welcoming, with all my
past mistakes oppressing it, and
showing me distorted forms
of fear?

Yet in the present love is obvious,
and its effects apparent.

All the world shines in reflection of its
holy light, and I perceive a
world forgiven at last.

Workbook-p II. Lesson 293. 1:1-5.

OCTOBER 21

Health is the result of
relinquishing all attempts to use
the body lovelessly.

Text-8. VIII. 9:9.

OCTOBER 22

The
Holy
Spirit
looks
through
me
today.

Workbook-p II. Lesson 295.

OCTOBER 23

The
Holy
Spirit
speaks
through
me
today.

Workbook-p II. Lesson 296.

OCTOBER 24

Forgiveness is the only gift I give,
because it is the only gift
I want.

And everything I give
I give myself.

This is salvation's simple
formula.

Workbook-p II. Lesson 297. 1:1-3.

OCTOBER 25

Father, I come to You today,
because I would not follow any
way but Yours. You are beside
me. Certain is Your way. And I
am grateful for Your holy gifts
of certain sanctuary, and escape
from everything that would
obscure my love for God my
Father and His holy Son.

Workbook-p II. Lesson 298. 2:1-4.

OCTOBER 26

Eternal
holiness
abides
in
me.

Workbook-p II. Lesson 299.

OCTOBER 27

Nothing
you
can
do
can
change
Eternal
Love.

Manual for Teachers. Clarification of Terms. 5. 6:10.

OCTOBER 28

And
God
Himself
shall
wipe
away
all
tears.

Workbook-p II. Lesson 301.

OCTOBER 29

When you
want
only love
you will
see
nothing
else.

Text-12. VII. 8:1.

OCTOBER 30

Watch with me, angels, watch
with me today.

Let all God's holy Thoughts
surround me, and be still with me
while Heaven's Son is born.

Let earthly sounds be quiet, and
the sights to which I am
accustomed disappear.

Let Christ be welcomed where
He is at home.

And let Him hear the sounds He
understands, and see but sights that
show His Father's Love.

Let Him no longer be a stranger here,
for He is born again
in me today.

Workbook-p II. Lesson 303. 1:1-6.

OCTOBER 31

Perception is a mirror,
not a fact.

And what I look on is my
state of mind, reflected
outward.

I would bless the world by
looking on it through the
eyes of Christ.

Workbook-p II. Lesson 304. 1:3-5.

NOVEMBER

NOVEMBER 1

Father,
the peace of Christ
is given us, because
it is Your Will that we
be saved. Help us
today but to accept
Your gift, and judge
it not. For it has
come to us to save
us from our
judgment on
ourselves.

Workbook-p II. Lesson 305. 2:1-3.

NOVEMBER 2

What but Christ's vision would
I use today, when it can offer me
a day in which I see a world so like
to Heaven that an ancient memory
returns to me?

Today I can forget the world I made.
Today I can go past all fear, and
be restored to love and holiness
and peace.

Today I am redeemed, and born anew
into a world of mercy and of care;
of loving kindness and the
peace of God.

Workbook-p II. Lesson 306. 1:1-4.

NOVEMBER 3

Nothing is difficult
that is *wholly*
desired.

Text-6. VB. 8:7.

NOVEMBER 4

The birth of Christ is now,
without a past or future.

He has come to give His
present blessing to the world,
restoring it to timelessness
and love.

And love is ever-present,
here and now.

Workbook-p II. Lesson 308. 1:6-8.

NOVEMBER 5

The Holy Spirit's Voice
is as loud as your
willingness
to listen.

Text-8. VIII. 8:7.

NOVEMBER 6

*This day, my Father, would I
spend with You, as You
have chosen all my days
should be. And what I will
experience is not of time
at all. The joy that comes to
me is not of days nor hours,
for it comes from Heaven
to Your Son. This day will be
Your sweet reminder to
remember You, Your gracious
calling to Your holy Son, the
sign Your grace has come to
me, and that it is Your Will
I be set free today.*

Workbook-p II. Lesson 310. 1:1-4.

NOVEMBER 7

This is God's Final Judgment:

"You are still My holy Son,
forever innocent,
forever loving
and forever loved,
as limitless as your
Creator, and completely
changeless and
forever pure.

Therefore awaken and
return to Me.

I am your Father
and you are
My Son."

Workbook-p II. Lesson 310. 10. 5:1-3.

NOVEMBER 8

Look once again upon your brother,
not without the understanding that
he is the way to Heaven or to hell,
as you perceive him.

But forget not this;
the role you give to him is given you,
and you will walk the way you pointed
out to him because it is your
judgment on yourself.

Text-25. V. 6:5-6.

NOVEMBER 9

Let us today behold each other
in the sight of Christ.

How beautiful we are!

How holy and how loving!

Brother, come and join with
me today.

We save the world when we
have joined.

For in our vision it becomes as
holy as the light
in us.

Workbook-p II. Lesson 313. 2:1-6.

NOVEMBER 10

Fear is not of the present,
but only of the past and future,
which do not exist.

There is no fear in the present
when each instant stands clear and
separated from the past, without its
shadow reaching out into
the future.

Each instant is a clean,
untarnished birth, in which the
Son of God emerges from
the past into the present.

And the present extends forever.

It is so beautiful and so clean and
free of guilt that nothing but
happiness is there.

No darkness is remembered, and
immortality and joy are now.

Text-15. I. 8:2-7.

NOVEMBER 11

Each day a thousand treasures come to me
with every passing moment.

I am blessed with gifts throughout the day,
in value far beyond all things of which
I can conceive.

A brother smiles upon another, and
my heart is gladdened.

Someone speaks a word of gratitude or mercy,
and my mind receives this gift and
takes it as its own.

And everyone who finds the way to God
becomes my savior, pointing out the way
to me, and giving me his certainty that
what he learned is surely
mine as well.

Workbook-p II. Lesson 315. 1:1-5.

NOVEMBER 12

His grace is given me in every
gift a brother has received
throughout all time, and past
all time as well.

My treasure house is full, and
angels watch its open doors
that not one gift is lost, and
only more are added.

Let me come to where my
treasures are, and enter in
where I am truly welcome
and at home, among the
gifts that God has
given me.

Workbook-p II. Lesson 316. 1:3-5.

NOVEMBER 13

Trust would settle
every problem
now.

Text-26. VIII. 2:3.

NOVEMBER 14

I am the means
by which God's Son is saved
because salvation's purpose is
to find the sinlessness that God
has placed in me.

I was created as the thing
I seek.

I am the goal the world is
searching for.

I am God's Son, His one
eternal Love.

I am salvation's means
and end as well.

Workbook-p II. Lesson 318. 1:4-8.

NOVEMBER 15

The ego thinks that what one gains,
totality must lose.

And yet it is the Will of God I learn
that what one gains is
given unto all.

Workbook-p II. Lesson 319. 1:5-6.

NOVEMBER 16

The Son of God is limitless.

There are no limits on his strength,
his peace, his joy, nor any attributes
his Father gave in his creation.

What he wills with his Creator and
Redeemer must be done.

His holy will can never be denied,
because his Father shines upon
his mind, and lays before it all
the strength and love in earth
and Heaven.

I am he to whom all this is given.

I am he in whom the power of my
Father's Will abides.

Workbook-p II. Lesson 320. 1:1-6.

NOVEMBER 17

The freedom to leave behind everything
that hurts you and humbles you
and frightens you cannot be thrust
upon you, but it can be offered you
through the grace of God.

And you can accept it by His grace,
for God is gracious to His Son,
accepting him without question
as His Own.

Text-11. VI. 6:3-4.

NOVEMBER 18

There is nothing outside you.

That is what you must ultimately learn,
for it is the realization that the
Kingdom of Heaven is restored
to you.

For God created only this, and He did
not depart from it nor leave it separate
from Himself.

The Kingdom of Heaven is the
dwelling place of the Son of God, who
left not his Father and dwells not apart
from Him.

Heaven is not a place nor a condition.
It is merely an awareness of perfect
Oneness, and the knowledge that
there is nothing else; nothing outside
this Oneness, and nothing else
within.

Text-18. VI. 1:1-6.

NOVEMBER 19

Here is the only "sacrifice" You ask
of Your beloved Son; You ask him
to give up all suffering, all sense of
loss and sadness, all anxiety and
doubt, and freely let Your Love
come streaming in to his
awareness, healing him of pain,
and giving him Your Own eternal
joy. Such is the "sacrifice" You ask
of me, and one I gladly make; the
only "cost" of restoration of Your
memory to me, for the salvation
of the world.

Workbook-p II. Lesson 323. 1:1-2.

NOVEMBER 20

*Father, You are the One Who
gave the plan for my salvation to
me. You have set the way I am
to go, the role to take, and every
step in my appointed path. I
cannot lose the way. I can but
choose to wander off a while,
and then return. Your loving
Voice will always call me back,
and guide my feet aright. My
brothers all can follow in the
way I lead them. Yet I merely
follow in the way to You, as
You direct me and would
have me go.*

Workbook-p II. Lesson 324. 1:1-7.

NOVEMBER 21

This is salvation's keynote:

What I see reflects a process in
my mind, which starts with my idea
of what I want.

From there, the mind makes up
an image of the thing the mind
desires, judges valuable, and
therefore seeks to find.

These images are then projected
outward, looked upon, esteemed as
real and guarded as
one's own.
From insane wishes comes
an insane world.

From judgment comes a
world condemned.

And from forgiving thoughts a
gentle world comes
forth . . .

Workbook-p II. Lesson 325. 1:1-6.

NOVEMBER 22

*Father, I was created in Your
Mind, a holy Thought that never
left its home. I am forever Your
Effect, and You forever and
forever are my Cause. As You
created me I have remained.
Where You established me I still
abide. And all Your attributes
abide in me, because it is Your
Will to have a Son so like his
Cause that Cause and Its Effect
are indistinguishable.*

Workbook-p II. Lesson 326. 1:1-5.

NOVEMBER 23

Love always answers,
being unable to deny a call for help,
or not to hear the cries of pain that
rise to it from every part of this
strange world you made
but do not want.

Text-13. VII. 4:3.

NOVEMBER 24

It is only because you think that
you can run some little part,
or deal with certain aspects
of your life alone,
that the guidance
of the Holy Spirit
is limited.

Text-14. XI. 8:4.

NOVEMBER 25

*Father, I thought I wandered
from Your Will, defied it, broke
its laws, and interposed a second
will more powerful than Yours.
Yet what I am in truth is but
Your Will, extended and
extending. This am I, and this
will never change. As You are
One, so am I one with You. And
this I chose in my creation,
where my will became forever
one with Yours. That choice was
made for all eternity. It cannot
change, and be in opposition to
itself. Father, my will is Yours.
And I am safe, untroubled and
serene, in endless joy, because
it is Your Will that it be so.*

Workbook-p II. Lesson 329. 1:1-9.

NOVEMBER 26

Healing is release from the
fear of waking and
the substitution of the
decision to wake.

The decision to wake is the
reflection of the will to love,
since all healing involves
replacing
fear
with
love.

Text-8. IX. 5:1-2.

NOVEMBER 27

*You love me, Father. You could
never leave me desolate, to die
within a world of pain and
cruelty. How could I think that
Love has left Itself? There is no
will except the Will of Love.
Fear is a dream, and has no will
that can conflict with Yours.
Conflict is sleep, and peace
awakening. Death is illusion;
life, eternal truth. There is no
opposition to Your Will. There
is no conflict, for my will
is Yours.*

Workbook-p II. Lesson 331. 1:3-11.

NOVEMBER 28

Fear
binds
the
world.

Forgiveness
sets
it
free.

Workbook-p II. Lesson 332.

NOVEMBER 29

Father, forgiveness is the light
You chose to shine away all
conflict and all doubt, and
light the way for our
return to You. No light but this
can end our evil dream. No
light but this can save the
world. For this alone will
never fail in anything,
being Your gift to Your
beloved Son.

Workbook-p II. Lesson 333. 2:1-4.

NOVEMBER 30

Today
I
claim
the
gifts
forgiveness
gives.

Workbook-p II. Lesson 334.

DECEMBER

DECEMBER 1

When a
brother behaves insanely,
you can heal him only by
perceiving the sanity
in him.

Text-9. III. 5:1.

DECEMBER 2

In quiet may forgiveness wipe away
my dreams of separation and of sin.
Then let me, Father, look within,
and find Your promise of my
sinlessness is kept; Your Word
remains unchanged within my
mind, Your Love is still
abiding in my heart.

Workbook-p II. Lesson 336. 2:1-2.

DECEMBER 3

My sinlessness ensures me
perfect peace, eternal safety, everlasting love,
freedom forever from all thought of loss;
complete deliverance from suffering.

And only happiness can be my state,
for only happiness is given me.

What must I do to know all this is mine?
I must accept Atonement for myself,
and nothing more.

Workbook-p II. Lesson 337. 1:1-4.

DECEMBER 4

The Thoughts of God are far beyond
all change, and shine forever.

They await not birth. They wait for
welcome and remembering.

The Thought God holds of you is like
a star, unchangeable in an
eternal sky.

So high in Heaven is it set that those
outside of Heaven know not
it is there.

Yet still and white and lovely will it
shine through all eternity.

There was no time it was not there;
no instant when its light grew
dimmer or less perfect
ever was.

Text-30. III. 8:1-7.

DECEMBER 5

Father, this is Your day.
It is a day in which I would
do nothing by myself, but
hear Your Voice in
everything I do;
requesting only what You
offer me, accepting only
Thoughts You share
with me.

Workbook-p II. Lesson 339. 2:1-2.

DECEMBER 6

Be glad today! Be glad!
There is no room for anything
but joy and thanks
today.

Our Father
has redeemed His Son
this day.

Not one of us but will be
saved today.

Not one who will remain in fear,
and none the Father will not gather
to Himself, awake in Heaven in
the Heart of Love.

Workbook-p II. Lesson 340. 2:1-6.

DECEMBER 7

Father, Your Son is holy. I am
he on whom You smile in love
and tenderness so dear and deep
and still the universe smiles
back on You, and shares Your
Holiness. How pure, how safe,
how holy, then, are we, abiding
in Your Smile, with all Your
Love bestowed upon us, living
one with You, in brotherhood
and Fatherhood complete; in
sinlessness so perfect that the
Lord of Sinlessness conceives
us as His Son, a universe of
Thought completing Him.

Workbook-p II. Lesson 341. 1:1-3.

DECEMBER 8

I let forgiveness rest upon
all things.

For thus forgiveness will be
given me.

Workbook-p II. Lesson 342.

DECEMBER 9

The mercy and
the peace of God
are free.

Salvation has no cost.

It is a gift that must be
freely given and
received.

And it is this that
we would learn
today.

Workbook-p II. Lesson 343. 2:1-4.

DECEMBER 10

Today
I learn the law of love;
that what
I give my
brother
is my
gift
to
me.

Workbook-p II. Lesson 344.

DECEMBER 11

I offer
only
miracles
today,
For I
would
have
them
be
returned
to
me.

Workbook-p II. Lesson 345.

DECEMBER 12

*Father, I wake today with miracles
correcting my perception of all
things. And so begins the day I
share with You as I will share
eternity, for time has stepped aside
today. I do not seek the things of
time, and so I will not look upon
them. What I seek today transcends
all laws of time and things perceived
in time. I would forget all things
except Your Love. I would abide in
You, and know no laws except Your
law of love. And I would find the
peace which You created for Your
Son, forgetting all the foolish toys I
made as I behold Your glory
and my own.*

Workbook-p II. Lesson 346. 1:1-7.

DECEMBER 13

Listen today.

Be very still, and
hear the gentle
Voice for God
assuring you
that He
has
judged
you
as
the
Son
He
loves.

Workbook-p II. Lesson 347. 2:1-2.

DECEMBER 14

*Father, let me remember You
are here, and I am not alone.
Surrounding me is everlasting
Love. I have no cause for
anything except the perfect
peace and joy I share with You.
What need have I for anger or
for fear? Surrounding me is
perfect safety. Can I be afraid,
when Your eternal promise goes
with me? Surrounding me is
perfect sinlessness. What can I
fear, when You created me in
holiness as perfect as Your
Own?*

Workbook-p II. Lesson 348. 1:1-8.

DECEMBER 15

Today I let Christ's vision look upon
All things for me and judge them not, but give
Each one a miracle of love instead.

Workbook-p II. Lesson 349.

DECEMBER 16

Learn this, and learn it well,
for it is here delay of happiness is
shortened by a span of time
you cannot realize.

You never hate your brother for his sins,
but only for your own.

Whatever form his sins appear to take,
it but obscures the fact that you
believe them to be yours, and
therefore meriting
a "just" attack.

Text-31. III. 1:4-6.

DECEMBER 17

My sinless brother is
my guide to
peace.

My sinful brother is
my guide to
pain.

And which I choose
to see I will
behold.

Workbook-p II. Lesson 351.

DECEMBER 18

Judgment and love
are opposites.

From one
come all the sorrows
of the world.

But
from the other
comes the
peace of God
Himself.

Workbook-p II. Lesson 352.

DECEMBER 19

*Father, I give all that is mine
today to Christ, to use in any
way that best will serve the
purpose that I share with Him.
Nothing is mine alone, for He
and I have joined in purpose.
Thus has learning come almost
to its appointed end. A while I
work with Him to serve His
purpose. Then I lose myself in
my Identity, and recognize that
Christ is but my Self.*

Workbook-p II. Lesson 353. 2:1-5.

DECEMBER 20

We stand together, Christ and I, in peace
And certainty of purpose. And in Him
Is His Creator, as He is in me.

Workbook-p II. Lesson 354.

DECEMBER 21

Prayer is
a way offered by the Holy Spirit
to reach God.

It is not merely a question
or an entreaty.

It cannot succeed until
you realize that it asks for nothing.

How else could it serve its purpose?

It is impossible to pray for idols
and hope to reach God.

True prayer must avoid the pitfall
of asking to entreat.

Ask, rather,
to receive what is already given;
to accept what is already there

Song of Prayer-1. I. 1:1-7.

DECEMBER 22

I must have decided wrongly,
because I am not at peace.

I made the decision myself,
but I can also decide otherwise.

I want to decide otherwise,
because I want to be at peace.

I do not feel guilty, because the
Holy Spirit will undo all the
consequences of my wrong
decision if I will let Him.

I choose to let Him, by allowing
Him to decide for
God for me.

Text-5. VII. 6:7-11.

DECEMBER 23

Teach no one that he is what
you would not want to be.

Your brother is the mirror in which
you see the image of yourself as
long as perception lasts.

Text-7. VII. 3:8-9.

DECEMBER 24

This Christmas
give the Holy Spirit everything
that would hurt you.

Let yourself be healed completely
that you may join with Him
in healing, and let us celebrate
our release together by
releasing everyone
with us.

Text-15. XI. 3:1-2.

DECEMBER 25

The sign of Christmas is a star,
a light in darkness.

See it not outside yourself, but
shining in the Heaven within,
and accept it as the sign
the time of Christ has
come.

He comes demanding nothing.
No sacrifice of any kind,
of anyone, is asked
by Him.

In His Presence the whole idea
of sacrifice loses all meaning.
For He is Host
to God.

Text-15. XI. 2:1-6.

DECEMBER 26

Father, it is Your peace that I
would give, receiving it of You.
I am Your Son, forever just as
You created me, for the Great
Rays remain forever still and
undisturbed within me. I would
reach to them in silence and in
certainty, for nowhere else can
certainty be found. Peace be
to me, and peace to all the world.
In holiness were we created, and
in holiness do we remain. Your
Son is like to You in perfect
sinlessness. And with this
thought we gladly say
"Amen."

Workbook-p II. Lesson 360. 1:1-7.

DECEMBER 27

The world will end in joy,
because it is a place of sorrow.
When joy has come, the purpose of
the world has gone.

The world will end in peace,
because it is a place of war.
When peace has come, what is
the purpose of the world?

The world will end in laughter,
because it is a place of tears.
Where there is laughter, who
can longer weep?

And only complete forgiveness
brings all this to bless
the world.

Manual for Teachers. 14. 5:1-7.

DECEMBER 28

You have reached the end of an ancient journey,
not realizing yet that it is over.

You are still worn and tired, and the desert's dust
still seems to cloud your eyes and
keep you sightless.

Yet He Whom you welcomed has come to you,
and would welcome you.

He has waited long to give you this.
Receive it now of Him, for He would have you
know Him.

Only a little wall of dust still stands between you
and your brother. Blow on it lightly and with
happy laughter, and it will fall away.

And walk into the garden love has prepared
for both of you.

Text-18. VIII. 13:1-8.

DECEMBER 29

This holy instant would I give to You.
Be You in charge. For I would follow You,
certain that Your direction gives me peace.

And if I need a word to help me,
He will give it to me.

If I need a thought,
that will He also give.

And if I need but stillness and
a tranquil, open mind, these are
the gifts I will receive of Him.

He is in charge by my request.
And He will hear and answer me,
because He speaks for God my
Father and His holy Son.

Workbook-p II. Lessons 361 to 365. 1:1-5.

DECEMBER 30

This course is a beginning, not an end.

Your Friend goes with you.
You are not alone.

No one who calls on Him can
call in vain.

Whatever troubles you,
be certain that He has the answer,
and will gladly give it to you,
if you simply turn to Him
and ask it of Him.

He will not withhold all answers
that you need for anything that
seems to trouble you. He knows
the way to solve all problems,
and resolve all doubts.

His certainty is yours.
You need but ask it of Him,
and it will be given
you.

Workbook-p II. Epilogue. 1:1-9.

DECEMBER 31

And now in all your doings be you blessed.
God turns to you for help to save the world.
Teacher of God, His thanks He offers you,
And all the world stands silent in the grace
You bring from Him. You are the Son He loves,
And it is given you to be the means
Through which His Voice is heard around the world,
To close all things of time; to end the sight
Of all things visible; and to undo
All things that change. Through you is ushered in
A world unseen, unheard, yet truly there.
Holy are you, and in your light the world
Reflects your holiness, for you are not
Alone and friendless. I give thanks for you,
And join your efforts on behalf of God,
Knowing they are on my behalf as well,
And for all those who walk to God with me.

AMEN

Manual For Teachers. 29. 8:1-8.

LIBRARY

A Course in Miracles, Foundation for Inner Peace, Combined Volume, Third Edition (2007).

Absence from Felicity: The Story of Helen Schucman and Her Scribing of A Course in Miracles, by Kenneth Wapnick, Foundation for A Course in Miracles (2nd edition 1991).

The Forgotten Song & The Song Remembered: The Story of A Course in Miracles, DVD, Foundation for Inner Peace (1987).

Gifts from A Course in Miracles, edited by Frances Vaughan, Ph.D., and Roger Walsh, M.D., Ph.D., Jeremy P. Tarcher/Putnam (1995).

A Return to Love: Reflections on the Principles of "A Course in Miracles," by Marianne Williamson, Harper Collins (1992).

The Miracle of Real Forgiveness, by Tom Carpenter's, Carpenter Press (2010).

Love is Letting Go of Fear, by Gerald G. Jampolsky, Celestial Arts (1982).

May Cause Miracles, by Gabrielle Bernstein, Harmony (2013).

Living A Course in Miracles: An Essential Guide to the Classic Text, by Jon Mundy, Ph.D., Sterling Ethos (2011).

Love Always Answers: Walking the Path of "Miracles," by Diane Berke, Crossroad (1994).

Understanding A Course in Miracles: The History, Message, and Legacy of a Spiritual Path for Today, by D. Patrick Miller, Celestial Arts (2008).

RESOURCES

A Course in Miracles has inspired a generation of philosophers, teachers, and authors. To find out more I recommend you contact one of the many national networks that features information on conferences and workshops, study groups, on-line courses, and multimedia publications based on or inspired by *A Course in Miracles*.

Foundation for *A Course in Miracles*
41397 Buecking Drive, Temecula, California 92590-5668
www.facim.org

Foundation for Inner Peace
PO Box 598 Mill Valley, CA 94942-0598
www.acim.org

Miracle Network
12a Barness Court, 6/8 Westbourne Terrace, London W2 3UW
www.miracles.org.uk

Miracle Distribution Center
3947 E. La Palma Avenue, Anaheim, California 92807
www.miraclecenter.org

Circle of Atonement
P.O. Box 4238, West Sedona, AZ 86340
www.circleofa.org

ACKNOWLEDGMENTS

A Course in Miracles has blessed my life and work. I am grateful to the many teachers who have helped me study and practice the essential principles of this sacred work. Thank you to Tom and Linda Carpenter for your shining example. Thank you Marianne Williamson for your inspiration. Thank you Nick Davis for your clarity. Thank you to Ken Wapnick, Chuck and Lency Spezzano, Alan Cohen, Gerry Jampolsky, and Sondra Ray for your great work. Thank you Ian Patrick for being Mr. Miracles in the UK.

Thank you to my family and friends. Thank you Hollie Holden for all your read-throughs and edits. I love studying the Course with you. Thank you everyone who has played a part in helping to learn and teach the Course, particularly Miranda Macpherson, who I ran my first study group with. "To teach is to learn," states the Course. Thank you to everyone who has hosted and attended one of my talks and workshops around the world.

Thank you to the Hay House team. Thank you to my editor, Patty Gift, for your vision and care in making *Holy Shift!* happen. Thank you Michelle Polizzi for your cover design, and Joan Duncan Oliver for your editing. Thank you to the William Morris Endeavour Entertainment, and especially to my agent, Jennifer Rudolph Walsh.

ABOUT THE AUTHOR

Robert Holden, Ph.D., is a student of *A Course in Miracles*. He is a Patron of the Miracle Network in the UK, founded in 1994. His innovative work on psychology and spirituality has been featured on *Oprah, Good Morning America*, a PBS show called *Shift Happens!* and two major BBC documentaries. He's the author of *Happiness NOW!, Authentic Success, Shift Happens!, Be Happy,* and *Loveability.* He contributes daily to his Facebook page (drrobertholden). He hosts a weekly show for Hay House Radio called *Shift Happens!*

www.robertholden.org

Hay House Titles of Related Interest

YOU CAN HEAL YOUR LIFE, the movie,
starring Louise Hay & Friends
(available as a 1-DVD program and an expanded 2-DVD set)
Watch the trailer at: www.LouiseHayMovie.com

THE SHIFT, the movie,
starring Dr. Wayne W. Dyer
(available as a 1-DVD program and an expanded 2-DVD set)
Watch the trailer at: www.DyerMovie.com

❖❖❖

ENOUGH ALREADY: The Power of Radical Contentment,
by Alan Cohen

*MIRACLES NOW: 108 Life-Changing Tools for Less Stress, More
Flow, and Finding Your True Purpose,* by Gabrielle Bernstein

*NURTURING HEALING LOVE: A Mother's Journey of Hope &
Forgiveness,* by Scarlett Lewis with Natasha Stoynoff

REVEAL: A Sacred Manual for Getting Spiritually Naked,
by Meggan Watterson

All of the above are available at your local bookstore,
or may be ordered by contacting Hay House (see next page).

We hope you enjoyed this Hay House book.
If you'd like to receive our online catalog featuring
additional information on Hay House books and products,
or if you'd like to find out more about the
Hay Foundation, please contact:

Hay House, Inc., P.O. Box 5100, Carlsbad, CA 92018-5100
(760) 431-7695 or (800) 654-5126
(760) 431-6948 (fax) or (800) 650-5115 (fax)
www.hayhouse.com® • www.hayfoundation.org

❖❖❖

Published and distributed in Australia by:
Hay House Australia Pty. Ltd., 18/36 Ralph St.,
Alexandria NSW 2015 • *Phone:* 612-9669-4299
Fax: 612-9669-4144 • www.hayhouse.com.au

Published and distributed in the United Kingdom by:
Hay House UK, Ltd., Astley House, 33 Notting Hill Gate,
London W11 3JQ • *Phone:* 44-20-3675-2450 •
Fax: 44-20-3675-2451 • www.hayhouse.co.uk

Published and distributed in the Republic of South Africa by:
Hay House SA (Pty), Ltd., P.O. Box 990, Witkoppen 2068
Phone/Fax: 27-11-467-8904 • www.hayhouse.co.za

Published in India by: Hay House Publishers India,
Muskaan Complex, Plot No. 3, B-2, Vasant Kunj,
New Delhi 110 070 • *Phone:* 91-11-4176-1620
Fax: 91-11-4176-1630 • www.hayhouse.co.in

Distributed in Canada by: Raincoast Books,
2440 Viking Way, Richmond, B.C. V6V 1N2 • *Phone:*
1-800-663-5714 • *Fax:* 1-800-565-3770 • www.raincoast.com

❖❖❖

<u>Take Your Soul on a Vacation</u>

Visit www.HealYourLife.com® to regroup, recharge,
and reconnect with your own magnificence.
Featuring blogs, mind-body-spirit news, and
life-changing wisdom from Louise Hay and friends.

Visit www.HealYourLife.com today!